LatinX

T0025158

Forerunners: Ideas First

Short books of thought-in-process scholarship, where intense analysis, questioning, and speculation take the lead

FROM THE UNIVERSITY OF MINNESOTA PRESS

(Continued on page 104)

LatinX

Claudia Milian

University of Minnesota Press
MINNEAPOLIS
LONDON

Portions of this book appeared in a different form as "Extremely Latin, XOXO: Notes on LatinX," in *Cultural Dynamics* 29, no. 3 (August 2017): 8–24, https://doi.org/10.1177/0921374017727850; and as "Crisis Management and the LatinX Child," in *English Language Notes* 56, no. 2 (October 2018): 121–40; copyright 2018, The Regents of the University of Colorado, a body corporate, all rights reserved, republished by permission of the copyright holder, and the present publisher, Duke University Press, www .dukeupress.edu.

Published by the University of Minnesota Press
111 Third Avenue South, Suite 290
Minneapolis, MN 55401–2520
http://www.upress.umn.edu

Available as a Manifold edition at manifold.umn.edu

The University of Minnesota is an equal-opportunity educator and employer.

Para mi madre, Betsy Arias, acompañándome y apoyándome en cada logro.

To Hampshire College (1970–2019+), where it all started.

Contents

Introduction

I'VE NEVER BEEN ABSOLUTELY CERTAIN what the frequently used terms Latina and Latino refer to. Or are. And I'm not particularly confident what LatinX is. Or means.

I can begin with a rather laconic personal genealogy: Salvadoran child is brought to the United States by her mother to live in West New York, New Jersey, or the "eternally dissed state of New Jersey," as artist and historian Nell Painter dubs it (2018, 11). Her town is located in Northern Jersey—colloquially known as the "Embroidery Capital of the World since 1872"—on Manhattan's fringes. She speaks Telemundo Spanish and comes of age alongside a mélange of Latin American nationalities, many of whom are casualties of the Cold War: Argentines, Brazilians, Chileans, Colombians, Cubans, Dominicans, Ecuadorans, Guatemalans, Hondurans, Mexicans, Nicaraguans, and Puerto Ricans, among other arrivals.

In my vintage years—which is to say, the closing decade of the twentieth century, and to some extent, the early twenty-first—I was reminded that I was part of what constituted "secondary Hispanic" status in the United States. I mention this designation not in judgment but simply to note that the Latina or Hispanic categories—their structuring and my assertion of them—have never been a ready and factual given.

I have observed and analyzed these labels and ontological claims from a distance, making sense of how—and when—Latina and Latino came into being and how these markers and states were understood and accepted, since my sociocultural and political experiences of this category were not deemed as a necessary condition of it. The question I have been invariably asking is:

how does one convey and theorize the contested terms of Latino/
Latina when—as my formal undergraduate education and graduate school training evinced—there were no academic or cultural
concepts that were applicable, or methodological, to my kind of
U.S. subject formation?

There was no representational content for (and of) Central
Americanness—not just as a geopolitical space, but also as some
kind of Latin conceptual experience in the United States (not to
mention its human circumstances and dimensions). What I am
trying to say is this: mine was an early articulation of LatinX. The
X as one that is falling through the Latin cracks—the spaces between the o's and the a's, the conventional understandings of what
it means to be Latino or Latina.

My first book, *Latining America: Black-Brown Passages and the
Coloring of Latino/a Studies* (Milian 2013), is an exercise in trying to discern the excess of Latin bodies and their accompanying
signifiers. This work attempted to stitch together and to unstitch
geographies of Latinness from multiple sites. I sought to grasp the
magnitude of what the slash in Latino/a or Latina/o meant, as well
as the @ sign in Latin@. The semiotics of the slash, the @, and now
the X have been standing together with another consistent label:
Latin. LatinX is a harbinger of two compounded configurations—
Latin *and* X—dual directional levels of signification. LatinX suggests a break—a force that requires a synthesis of joining Latin and
X, which complicates and makes space for discussions that do not
solely rely on binary configurations.

Latino/a has hardly functioned as an equivalent for nationality in
my uprooted world of the northern Garden State, which has stood
for Manhattan's margins, an epicenter of the hemisphere's deracinated entities. For years, it has provided the City that Never Sleeps
with surplus Latin labor, moving underground, in Manhattan's sub-
ways, in a space of unknowability, of transitions, of crossings: the
ultimate X. It is always a site of adulteration, of a fractured Latin
and X that could emerge and be substituted by any extricated Latin
body. A LatinX body does not necessitate extensive evidence of

its arrival point to, and presence in, the United States—or, for that matter, anywhere in the Global South's shiftiness.

This exposition is undergirded by three pillars of thought—three fundamental anchors inscribed by a futurity implicating our dire contemporary moment: LatinX, the Global South, and ecological devastation. This triad encompasses displacement as well as a speculative subjectivity, a theoretical geography, and the instability of climate change, all coupled with human adaptation to the new laws of nature. These modes of thought work through unexpected linkages from populations and canons of knowledge currently underway.

I understand that the intrinsic significance of the gender-neutral LatinX category speaks to inclusivity and fluidity. Nuyorican journalist Ed Morales wrote in the *Guardian* that LatinX "represents a queering of Latino" (2018b). Morales elaborated that he "embrace[s] Latinx because of its futurist implications. Like superheroes of color and the possibilities inherent in girls and everyone else who code, Latinx represents an openness that is increasingly under threat in a political climate that is most intent on drawing borders, keeping outsiders out, and using violence to keep it that way" (2018b). LatinX makes complete sense to me in that it offers a bigger environment to work with. LatinX has a very busy life. You can't pin down the Latin or the X: they both possess inherent hidden qualities and ubiquity in the world. LatinX delivers us to great unknowns.

Social scientists have spilled considerable ink on the emergence and function of the term Latino/a in the United States. While some academics have highlighted the category's top-down imposition by the mass media and the federal government on to a heterogeneous population, others have stressed the bottom-up process of self-naming, community formation, and panethnic identification (see Mora 2014; Beltrán 2010; De Genova and Ramos-Zayas 2003; Dávila 2001; Oboler 1995). It is assumed that Latino/a started—or peaked—in the late twentieth century. Yet historians increasingly point to the category's earlier circulation from the 1920s to 1970s (*vide* Contreras 2019; Cordova 2017; Fernández 2012; Thomas 2010). Latino/a has been generally employed to reference an amalgamation of peoples of Latin American descent; a U.S. ethnoracial identity and location; cultural connection and similitude; and political solidarity across ethnic nationalist affiliations.

I am partial to LatinX because it shows that Latino/a imaginations are not extinguished, that the terms Latina and Latino are not so "common sense" and complacent, after all. It shows that each LatinX handles and navigates the ontological category differently. And, yes, as Morales champions, LatinX sounds like the future. But it also holds the past and present. LatinX is a mixing and experiencing of these three categories, just as François Hartog frames historical time in our contemporary period and our openness toward the future (2015, xv). LatinX clues us in to how LatinXness is unfolding in the historical realities of our time. It gestures toward the exploration of the world—or an unknown, perhaps even hostile future—more fully and possibly more humbly.

The very enunciation of LatinX sounds strange—intimating dislocation and equivocation—and, as theorist Antonio Viego posits, "one hears LatinX; one cannot say that one sees LatinX" (2017, 163). This exogenous X comes from somewhere, anywhere—an elsewhere that is characterized with profound discrepancies. It forces us to probe into the story of LatinX's beginnings—not as linear but as processes of starting over and over again and challenging as well as interrogating its origins. To quote interdisciplinary artist R. Galvan, LatinX impels "continuous replenishment" (2017, 190).

What is a LatinX genealogy? What is its chronology? What sustains it? What has made it, and what makes it continuous? Must LatinXs and LatinXness inevitably be folded into "Latinidad"?

Stay with me. The questions shift and expand. What is LatinX? What are its horizons? Where is it dwelling, and where might it be moving? X's unknowability may signal that all Latin bodies are collapsed into that signifier, which begs the question: what is distinct within a LatinX Latinidad?

My interpretation presents a critical framework for LatinX's usefulness and pitfalls. This work is not about LatinX identity formation, or an ethnographic rendering of individuals who may or may not identify as LatinX. This scrutiny is also not a genealogical account—or, a full-scale cultural and intellectual history—of all the U.S. ethnoracial labels that have been affixed to Latina, Latino, or "Latin" populations. Nor is this undertaking a definitive statement, a nailed-down explication, or a flat-out resolution of the LatinX category and its proper pronunciation. Its enunciation, in either English or Spanish, varies along these lines: Lah-teen-ex (the accepted standard articulation); Lah-teenks (the frequent metathesistic mispronunciation); or Lah-teen-eh-kees (the admittance of the Spanish sound for the letter X).

LatinX does not have a country or fixed geography. But we might say that it is a "nation" of deracination. Even if we do know what and where LatinX is, we do not entirely know how to express or grasp it, or to manifestly say what it means.

LatinX unavoidably casts a shadow over the present. I gather what is available at this moment, the X, taking LatinX's "X" as a fruitful incitation, contemplation, and speculation––an urgent hermeneutic necessity for today. Its unifying problematic and interpretable features are linked by crises of the moment: "breaking" news and everyday events, instability, and projected catastrophic disasters and loss, as well as rapid change and disorientation that analytically put us to work.

This short book sorts out questions about being thrown into what can be understood as a LatinX critical state of affairs, not only in the contemporary moment, but also through the unknowability of social realities that exceed our present knowledge. These LatinX iterations are assessed, in some ways, through the vulnerable presence, the what-ifs, the trajectories, and the extreme inclusions and exclusions of unaccompanied Central American minors and climate change. LatinX garners meaning through these extant illustrations—through these flashes of crises—that mark acute violence and difference. But LatinX is not a Central American ontological embodiment or a satisfactory walking definition of LatinX.

I find LatinX's fundamental and capricious arbitrariness an invitation to further inquiry that remains open to possibilities. LatinX anticipates deployment. There is no orderly or intelligible inside or outside. Xs are endless—and, seemingly, so are the flows of Latins. LatinX is tinged with doubt. It is allopatric and generates a continuous rethinking of networks and relations. X assemblages reconstitute themselves. X is a possibility for exploring the unknown and the peculiar and for thinking through new political moments, geographies outside the Americas, and subject formations.

LatinX's ascendancy allows us to think about X not merely as a trend or as something to be in favor of or against, but as a point of orientation that allows us to start charting the realm of Latin*X* inquiry. LatinX, it seems to me, rearranges our Latino/a dictionary—our largely U.S.-situated lexicon—and moves to other conceptual histories, spaces, and perspectives.

LatinX plunges into what is currently happening and what may be coming. Its primacy—a present tense based on a quotidianness that reverberates in the future—is simultaneously in conversation with the tensions, iterations, and situations that make X possible. This book contours against pathways that LatinX, as a theoretical approach, begins to make seen. The intellectual possibilities for an unapologetic and urgent X worldview are realized alongside a nascent and developing LatinXness. Primary and secondary sources for LatinX approaches and epistemologies are unraveling. This monograph's X is transported to the uncertain, to what may be anticipated, as well as to present occurrences and conditions, near and far, that unsettle and compel us to submit to new sensibilities and ways of thinking. Sociologists Alex Wilkie, Martin Savransky, and Marsha Rosengarden call this mode of inquiry and its connection to futurity "speculative research" (2017). This framework bolsters my search for "something" that is "X": analytic patterns, processes of becoming, transformations, and the problematics of the present.

The LatinX moment invites us to think creatively, innovatively, and speculatively, building from the centrality—excessiveness even—of X. If we thought we knew all too well the o/a of the familiar Latino/a, LatinX tells us that things are no longer the same, that there is no secure footing, that the X—an expounding concept—is bound to new bodies and new schools of thought. No rigid definitions characterize this study. Illustrative examples, cultural representations and forms of expression, sociopolitical conjunctures, conceptual landscapes, and discourse analysis all proffer meaning-in-context. Describing and fleshing out how LatinX comes into view and into play figure prominently within these pages.

LatinX has propelled me to pursue and build on topics of inquiry that are affecting the field here and now. What does it mean, I ask, to be in this Latino/a Studies moment where we avail ourselves of the most current research through Latin*X* Studies? What are we doing with the ethical and political uncertainty of X? This is another way of asking: how are we encountering X, how is it impacting our research practices, what and where are our X sources, and what kinds of vocabularies are being generated through the X as methodology?

LatinX's advent is tackled here not as a synonym or a substitute for the Latino/a, Latina/o, or Latin@ ethnoracial and political descriptor. LatinX moves through dislocation, awkwardness, and illegitimacy. "Articulations," this book's first chapter, explores the fragments, differences, and discursive components chiseling X. X's present-day movement is also in transit—recording a new formation of LatinX's beginnings through the abject Central American child migrant—which is a topic canvassed in the second chapter, "Forms." And it is a space where anything can happen: an amorphous X can frustrate, terrify, and flummox, as the concluding chapter, "Numerosities," takes stock of climate change, displacement, and migration.

LatinX, to be sure, is in need of more time for theoretical approaches and insights, more time to dream, more time to be.

Articulations

THE PROVENANCE of the LatinX term is different than the "Latin" ethnoracial classifications of the not-too-distant past, the Latino/a (or Latina/o) and Latin@ now limping toward senectitude. Whereas Latina/o and Latin@ put forth the ethical inclusion of gender within the Latina and Latino landscape, individuals and networks challenging the exclusion produced by rigid gender assignment and ethnoracial expectations have gravitated toward the LatinX configuration, which *Merriam-Webster* added to its dictionary in September 2018 (Schaub 2018).

A cadre of activists and news outlets has weighed in on the impetus for ungendering Spanish and the relationship among language, subjectivity, and inclusion (see Latino USA 2016). My intent is not to undermine or dismiss the X's usefulness and political logic for transgender and other queer-identifying individuals. "The use of the 'x' is really important to me," Chicanx performance artist Artemisa Clark told one venue. "The 'x' shows a development of broader Latinx movements, one more actively concerned with issues of gender and queerness" (Padilla 2016). As with Clark, this meditation is not about semantics. My scholarly and creative energies are far from attempting to get the X "straight." Alba Onofrio, a North Carolina activist, stressed in teleSUR's electronic pages that LatinX parallels the political use of queer, along the lines of: "'We are queer and we have a critique of the system, and we want to be entirely different and not just let in.' That's the same thing I hear happening with Latinx." Onoforio continues: "Having the 'x' is a way of acknowledging that politicization, even in writing it. It's like, 'Fuck the binary, I won't participate in that.' I'm not gonna take part in your 'o' or 'a,' you can't make me choose" (Jamal 2017).

Onoforio's observations extract what seems to be painfully clear and available to us in our digital moment: binary, a way of being, has invaded multiple aspects of our present day, from the gendered Latino or Latina, from digital profile to real-life presence, and from writer to reader. Isa Noyola, a program director at the Transgender Law Center, emphasizes that LatinX "is the remedy to the binary, to ignorance and limiting possibilities. It's what's on the other side of basicness" (Rivas 2017). For poet, visual artist, and ethnic studies scholar Alan Pelaez Lopez, the X visualizes the Latin American diaspora as both wound and the ongoing wounding of Latinidad (2018). Given its ascendancy, it behooves self-identified LatinXs and pundits, in and out of the academy, to unearth its workings from theoretical, ethnographic, and policy vantage points.

X is a matter for mathematicians, theorists, popular culture practitioners, medical professionals, artists, activists, and ever so many more. Terry Moore, polymath and director of the nonprofit organization the Radius Foundation, delivered a popular TED Talk viewed 3,677,765 times (and counting) entitled, "Why Is 'X' the Unknown?" (2012). The conceit of his thesis is that medieval Spanish scholars could not translate certain Arabic sounds such as the letter "sheen" (or, "shin"). X is the mathematical unknown "because you can't say 'sh' in Spanish." The X is not self-evident, as there is already some mathematical problem at work that must be solved empirically. And yet the X as praxis, as Moore notes, is "everywhere in our culture," underscoring that there is no burden of proof in forging a nexus with the X in everyday contexts.

Recall, for brevity's sake, this X storehouse charting various material culture clues: X Prize; X Games; Xbox; Xs and Os, or tic-tac-toe; the X and O wings of "the infamous maximum security cell blocks" where prison activist and Black Panther Party member George Jackson "and others had been incarcerated" (Treviño 2001,183); the epistolary tradition of ending love letters with XOXO for hugs and kisses; an X as a sign for college admission, or the likelihood of acceptance, such as the one a young

Sonia Sotomayor uncovered in a postcard from Princeton prior to being appointed U.S. Supreme Court Justice (2013, 118); the X street markings approximating where, in 1963, President John F. Kennedy was assassinated in Dallas's Dealey Plaza; the Roman numeral X; the Los Angeles punk rock group X; the English band the xx (and while jamming to their music, imbibing Dos Equis lagers); XXXX as a substitute for a four-letter swear word; a shady X rating for material to be viewed by adults only; an acne cleanser branded as X Out; XS or XL to abbreviate garment size specifications; X-rays and, as one may say for extraordinary human eyesight, X-ray vision; the X chromosome; SpaceX, the American aerospace manufacturer; "Desert X," the outdoor art exhibition in the Coachella Valley; Marvel's X-Men mutant superheroes and their X-filled world featuring Professor X, the X-Mansion, the X-Gene; *The X Files*; *Project X*; *The X Factor*; *American History X*; TEDx; Generation X, that body of individuals that, in author Kurt Vonnegut's ready wit, is "two clicks away from the very end of the alphabet" (1994); and, as U.S. Latina and Latino sociopolitical identities evince nowadays, LatinX.

Unlike Latino/a, LatinX's linguistic details intimate that they are echoes reflecting everywhere. Hence my reason for capitalizing the X at the term's end: LatinX synchs up, not so sotto voce, with a multitude of discourses and signifiers already in the public eye. The dual-directional semiotics demand a double process of disentanglement for Latin and the X. To step into LatinX being and LatinX spaces means to be as much Latin as X, for as Roland Barthes might put it, X is the sign of our social and ethnoracial world, and it marks our behavior in it. The LatinX horizon bumps up against so many daily uses in a way that Latino/a does (or did) not. There is almost nothing to break down: Latin is occupying a plethora of things in this munificent "X" gathering. One could not, as a case in point, readily "see" the labels Latina and Latino in, say, the Xbox (or, "LatinXbox," if you wish). The X also stands for anonymity, as when indigenous groups "signed over" their property and land rights to colonizing Europeans, or when Malcolm X claimed the symbol as an action of interpellation to be admitted into American society. LatinX conveniently appears to slide in as it moves "the" Latina and Latino out of the way.

But is it a sticky term? Is it a theoretical breakthrough? Does the X turn into our "common" language? And what does it mean when social and political problems with gender are not enunciated—when they are somehow not being attended to through LatinX, even as gender served as the catalyst for the move toward LatinX?

Previously, the distinction of the o/a in Latino/a was being forced into English discourse. Replacing the o/a in Latin with an X pushes these subjectivities far away. Both transgender and cisgender individuals are now, on the face of it, equally LatinX. And yet this is the reason there is both skepticism and excitement for a term like LatinX. It is restive and hard to pin down, and it pushes against those things we thought we knew and understood.

The very appellation of Latino/a, Latina/o, Latin@, and LatinX Studies speaks to the field's open-endedness. The intellectual language that frames Latino/a Studies at the institutional level enunciates and references the tensions and instability of Latina and Latino embodiments in its multiple iterations. Ironically the one static "thing" that stands "there"—unasked—is another gender-neutral term, centuries-old, with its own problematic conundrum: "Latin." The approaches to the queries just raised—what LatinX is, or can be—indeed vary and are evolving. They motivate us to keep open a sense of intellectual curiosity, or "the philosophy of curiosity," as Ilhan Inan puts it (2012).

This conceptual exploration raises a host of questions along the way. It is a thinking piece that rhetorically performs attempts at coming to know something. I delve into the instability of the matter: to feel the pulse on the open X-ness of it all as well as the abstractions and motley connections that are happening with this new signifier. My recurrent concerns are a way of going about something larger—a philosophical unknown where the interrelated questions being asked could be approached differently and reworked—well beyond these pages' scope. Scrutiny admits discursive engagement: it is a method of contemplation that encourages people to be part of the conversation because they are, after all, part of this analytic endeavor. Building on questions, as translator Edith Grossman postulates, peg "the almost impenetrable difficulty of a subject" (2010, 5–6).

X-Bodies: Symbolic Locations of the X

Long before LatinX's extant materialization, Chicana and Chicano ethnoracial articulations of "X-bodies," to borrow from cultural theorist Scott Bukatman (1994), attest that the X has been a significant precursor to the exploration of self-naming and of going from being an "un-identified" group to new political subjects. An abridged tally of Chicana and Chicano orientations toward the X illuminates, as historian Arturo F. Rosales summarizes, that the category "derived from the ancient Nahuatl word *mexicano* with the 'x' being pronounced as a 'shh' sound" (1997, 261). Feminist activist and playwright Cherríe Moraga makes known that she motions toward "Xicana and Xicano with an X (the Nahuatl spelling of the 'ch' sound) to indicate a re-emerging política, especially among young people, grounded in Indigenous American belief systems and identities" (2011, xxi). Together with those denominations, the distinction of MeXicanas and MeXicanos arises in Moraga's *A Xicana Codex of Changing Consciousness,* a collection of essays and poems published in 2011. In it, the X "reflects the Indian identity that has been robbed from us through colonization, akin to Malcolm X's use of the letter in place of his 'slave' name [. . .] As many Raza may not know their specific indigenous nation of origin, the X links us as Native people in diaspora" (xxi). Per critic Juan Velasco, this symbol has fashioned "a performative model of subjectivity through the recuperation and reconstruction of 'X' as a signifier of the Indian" (1996, 226).

In 1984's *The House on Mango Street*, poet and novelist Sandra Cisneros ascribed the X to the young Esperanza, who desires to begin afresh through an alias. Therein, Esperanza christens herself as "Zeze the X": "a name more like the real me, the one nobody sees" (13). Hers is not a perfect designation, but "something" that "will do." The "Zeze"/seesee alliteration carves out a moniker with a personal value, an X identifiable to—and voiced by—the self, and perhaps mirrored by "the other," the reader who must pronounce Zeze the X's "funny" name. Writer Ana Castillo proposed, in 1994, the term Xicanisma as an approach to Chicana feminism that would "allow for self-evaluation" through one's "indigenous connection to the Americas" and perspectives (161, 6). Xicanisma— or, "Xicanista" as Roberto Rodríguez, author of the syndicated "Column of the Americas" for Universal Press Syndicate, speaks of it—is "a fusion between Chicanas, feministas, and activistas" (1996, 7). Castillo's Xicanisma strives "to understand ourselves in the world, it may also help others who are not of Mexican background or women. It is yielding and based on integration, not dualisms" (1994, 166). Her frame of reference aspired to be "carried out to our work places, social gatherings, kitchens, bedrooms, and the public sphere" (21).

In 1996, Rodríguez self-published *The X in La Raza: An Anti-Book*. The X rewrites "problems of representation around new notions of difference" (Velasco 1996, 220). Rodríguez's X elicits Xicano participation "in indigenous networks throughout the Americas, particularly in support of the Zapatistas," thus forming the "X generation" (6, 8). On the Mexican literary front, author, philosopher, and diplomat Alfonso Reyes penned, in 1951, *La X en la frente* (or, "X on the Forehead") alluding to the enigmatic homeland and national challenges as an X. "Once you bring up the question of the X," Reyes remarked, "you open the problem. The word Mexico: should it be written with an x or a j?" (129; my translation).

Philological concerns aside, Reyes's X functions as a crossing of planes and roads. He deems it "as a historical relic, a discreet sign" that allows Mexicans "to recognize each other thanks to that X on the forehead" as a cultural identifier (Molina 2012; my translation). The X on the forehead potentially evokes the popular expression, or indictment, by Mexicans to Mexicans of having *"el nopal en la frente*," or "a cactus on the forehead." This negative saying, a projection of origins and value, is uttered when someone does not recognize or denies one's "authentic" Mexicanness. While we all understand what a cactus is, we do not share its cultural meaning. If the forehead's X designates a symbolic location, it depends on others to confirm that it is there, as no one can see what is on their forehead. The correlative to the cultural meaning of cactus is that otherness, rather than the self, determines it. The self is minimized in this transaction because the X on the forehead is mutable.

Literary critic Gloria Elizabeth Chacón lays out how LatinX unfolds for indigenous Mesoamerican populations and their presupposed fixed—and "non-alphabetic" in the Western sense—recognizability. LatinX "troubles ways of knowing and what is known about the Indian." The X's explicit shape (its slashes) infer "a violent juxtaposition of two different temporalities, calendars, and historical genealogies. The X makes a return to the sixteenth-century use of the Latin language, when, during this 'LatinX moment,' the X's phoneme expanded to represent an indigenous language sound. It is a confrontation between the Latin and indigenous languages—a 'mother tongue' that refuses gendered language. Feminine/masculine articles don't exist in Maya or Zapotec. But this does not mean that gendered ideologies are nonexistent." X is not a facile substitute but a collision evoking a presence, old and new. It is a powerful reminder that this X is sayable in the present tense and cannot fade. Under Chacón's premise, "The X is the ineffable indigenous language that keeps returning, a spontaneous 'speech' that attempts to resemanticize the Indian that has been physically, sexually, culturally, nationally, and geographically crossed—X'ed—out. Still, LatinX can also be an ethical position that engages with indigenous populations—X's—that are implicated everywhere in the US Latino/a worlds and its 'others.'" LatinX, as a shared signifier moving back and forth, is an opening toward social affiliations and political allegiances (Chacón 2019, 51–52).

Some scholars bemoan LatinX's overuse and misuse, appraising it as "an elitist attempt to erase a history of more traditional gender roles, or as a distraction from other pressing issues facing Latinos in the United States" (Nuño-Pérez and Aviles 2019). This rift downplays how LatinXness can partake in ethical demands and dilemmas, political emergencies, care for society, and higher intellectual pursuits. For Houston-based writer and performer Josh Inocéncio, LatinX's X "Anglicizes (i.e., whitewashes)" Latinas and Latinos. He advocates, instead, for another alternative term, "Latine," with an emphasis on the "e." Latine, under his scope of interest, "is more consistent with Spanish pronunciations and is gender neutral" (2017). U.S. LatinXs are positioned as this identifier's primary users, imposing it on the Hispanophone Americas.

But as the Spanish international news agency EFE has reported, both the X and the e are employed in the region's evolving linguistic landscape. The wire service has written that these letters' prevalence—gaining much traction in nations like Argentina—is driven by the feminist movement, transgender communities, and youth to include dissidences. Schools employ gender-neutral Xs and e's. One EFE source declared, "the reality is that most of the teachers speak with the 'e' and write with the 'x.' Many of the students' tests are written in an inclusive language" (EFE 2019). *Infobae*, an online Argentine news outlet, headlined this debate on genderless Spanish, asking, "Is the Spanish Language Sexist?: The Debate about the 'at' Sign, the X, and Sexist Terms" (Benavides 2018). The Royal Academy of Spanish (RAE), the world's largest institution safeguarding the language's proper uses, has unequivocally dismissed any word ending with an X, @, or e (Jenner 2018). Hark back to this rather persnickety RAE tweet: "It is not permissible to use the letter 'x' or 'e' as a gender mark. It is also unnecessary, since the masculine grammar works in our language, as in others, as an inclusive term to refer to mixed collectives, or in generic or nonspecific contexts" (January 22, 2018).

To quote journalist Socorro Carrillo, LatinX "is equal parts social-media firestorm, social movement, and social divider" in the United States (2016). The millennial-targeted website Fusion—a digital space the *Atlantic* calls "the corporate 'Frankenbaby' of

ABC and Univision" (Meyer 2015)—"allows and champions the use of Latinx, but if an individual identifies as Latino or Latina, we honor that preference and identify them as such" (Rivas 2017). The *Huffington Post* employs LatinX as a term to collectively denote Latinas and Latinos, "rather than only those who identify as genderqueer" (Carrillo 2016). LatinX communicates gender disruption, veers toward gender neutrality, embraces fluidity and multiple geographies, and speaks to "a mix of different 'latinesque races'" (Reichard 2015).

LatinX, as a term and lifestyle, is being packaged—or, "coded"—and "sold" to U.S. and Latin American bicultural audiences. On October 3, 2018, Telemundo and E! News premiered a weekly thirty-minute entertainment, fashion, and celebrity gossip program, *Latinx Now!* Produced in both English and Spanish, *Latinx Now!* airs on E! News's and Telemundo Entretenimiento's YouTube channels. As an NBCUniversal executive commented, the show's formula strives "to bring relevant and engaging content to our GenM (millennial, multicultural, mobile) audience and offer more choices and flexibility" (Marti 2018). X—always updated and refreshed, with immediate access on the go—is the cultural climate of our time, marking the "things" that NBCUniversal's GenM is made of.

American Theatre magazine devoted a special section in 2016 to "Latinx Theatre in the U.S." It explained that while Latina/o has "never taken hold as a style in most publications," LatinX "has emerged as the most inclusive adjective for people of all gender expressions." Yet this edition pointed out that "Latinx makes a poor noun; though we've certainly heard people try, 'Latinx-es' doesn't exactly roll off the tongue. What's more, the indeterminacy of 'x,' which can sound inclusive in an adjective, feels somehow inhuman in a noun (person = x?)" (Weinert-Kendt). With this interrogation in mind, and in a context where undocumented migrants are dehumanized, the X does not necessarily present an option for liberation or self-realization in the American theater of our daily lives.

Recall the X utilized for railroad crossings and the different meanings and unnamable hauntings this dangerous mode of transportation may connote for unauthorized Central American migrants (see Martínez 2014). They board the freight trains known as the Beast en route to the United States from Mexico. The X-ing here is not really a crossing. It is an X-out, a crossing-out, a continuous embodiment of X: X as expulsion, expendability, being expunged. X can also mean the unfamiliar—X as a blank—as not having a crossing or many points in common. The "alienation or dislocation" that "*los otros* dreamers" find upon being deported—or returned—to some Latin American nations signals that "many of these young people have no childhood memories of Mexico, no immediate family in Mexico" (Anderson and Solis 2014, 13, 1). Scholar Jorge Huerta joked in *American Theatre* that "'Latinx' sounds like the name of a laxative ('Latinx—get all the shit out!')." Writer, director, and performer Raquel Amalzan told this same venue: "Latinx is a rejection of stereotypical representation and the limitations of the colonial past, and an attempt to move us into the future" (2016).

LatinX's deeper reaches are found, too, in the Ford Foundation's recent philanthropic work. In September 2016, the foundation partnered with acclaimed Cuban American conceptual artist Teresita Fernández to hold the U.S.–Latinx Arts Futures Symposium at its Manhattan headquarters, bringing together leading visual artists, museum directors, curators, and scholars. The hosts used the LatinX qualifier, Fernández punctuated, to avoid the "default term [that] often becomes masculine: 'Latino'" (Morton 2016). LatinX is part of "a 'linguistic revolution' that [. . .] is inclusive of the intersecting identities of Latin American descendants living in the U.S." Fernández gives attention to how "the term implies a new conversation, one that purposefully seeks to address the intersectionalities that Latinxs represent across race, class, and nonbinary gender. As an inclusive term, it also gives a very specific space to young Latinxs. [. . .] It was important [. . .] to frame the day's conversation around the future, which will be defined by this younger generation that relates more to the term 'Latinx' than to 'Latino/a'" (Morton 2016).

Academic tomes attest to the unfolding of a canonical lexicon for twenty-first century Latinas and Latinos. Historian Gary Y. Okihiro explicates in *Third World Studies: Theorizing Liberation* that he subscribes to LatinX as a "nongendered form of Latina/o that implicates race, gender, sexuality, class, and nation and their intersections" (2016, 173). Guest editors Macarena Gómez-Barris and Licia Fiol-Matta employed LatinX in their 2014 special issue of *American Quarterly* (or, *Las Américas Quarterly*) "to signal a route out of gender binaries and normativities we can no longer rehearse. From the South and in the borderlands, the 'x' turns away from the dichotomous, toward a void, an unknown, a wrestling with plurality, vectors of multi-intentionality, and the transitional meanings of what has yet to be seen" (504). Sociolinguist scholar Lourdes Torres, who edits the field journal *Latino Studies*, wrote that the first time LatinX appeared in the publication was in its first 2017 issue, employed in an article about urban fiction (284). Since then, she added, there has been an approximate 20 percent increase in the terminological use of LatinX in *Latino Studies* manuscripts.

Three special journal issues have sifted through LatinX as a label and as a research method: "LatinX Studies: Variations and Velocities" in *Cultural Dynamics* (Milian 2019, 31.1–2); "Theorizing LatinX" in *Cultural Dynamics* (Milian 2017, 29.3); and "Latinx Lives in Hemispheric Context" in *English Language Notes (ELN)* (Windell and Alemán 2018, 56.2). Also consult, as brief illustrations, these titular LatinXs in Frederick Luis Aldama's edited volume, *Latinx Comic Book Storytelling: An Odyssey by Interview* (2016) and his coedited anthology with Christopher González, *Latinx Studies: The Key Concepts* (2019); Iris D. Ruiz and Raúl Sánchez's edited collection, *Decolonizing Rhetoric and Composition Studies: New Latinx Keywords for Theory and Pedagogy* (2016); Antonio (Jay) Pastrana, Juan Battle, and Angelique Harris's study, *An Examination of Latinx LGBT Populations across the United States: Intersections of Race and Sexuality* (2017); Patricia A. Ybarra's *Latinx Theater in the Times of Neoliberalism* (2017); Paul Ortiz's *An African American and Latinx History of the United States* (2018); Ralph E. Rodriguez's *Latinx Literature Unbound: Undoing*

Ethnic Expectation (2018); Ed Morales's *Latinx: The New Force of American Politics* (2018a); and Ricardo Ortiz's *Latinx Literature Now: Between Evanescence and Event* (2019).

Per *Inside Higher Ed,* LatinX is increasingly prevalent in university settings: "Google trend data show it began to appear in Internet searches" in 2015, and the label suddenly soared in November of that same year. "Experts say it first began to spread in academic literature about two years ago" (Logue 2015). And it's not just in the United States. LatinX's scale is circulating across the Atlantic. The London College of Fashion hosted the *Mundo LatinX* exhibition from February 8 to May 4, 2019, as a means to survey "the dominant narrative, played out in the media, that characterises Latin Americans as exotic, criminal and powerless" (Smyth 2019). Elizabeth Horan, a professor of English at Arizona State University, elucidates that LatinX "started in online chat rooms and listservs in the 1990s" (Rivas 2017). Fusion cites Horan as "the first to use the word" in a Fall 2004 volume of the journal *Feministas Unidas,* where the category "Latinx/@" surfaces (Rivas 2017; Horan 2004, 25).

The University of Denver offers a Certificate Program in LatinX Studies. The Yale University Library research guide highlights "the principal library resources for Latinx Studies" (guides.library .yale.edu). LatinX is "seen on protest signs and in names of student groups that ha[ve] historically included Latino in their names. Seattle University now has a Latinx Law Student Association, and Yale University's Divinity School has a Latinx and Latin American Christianity program. San Jose State University has a Chicanx/ Latinx Student Success Task Force" (Rivas 2017).

The University of California San Diego substituted the Latino and Chicano categories for Latinx and Chicanx. "The new word changes," the *Los Angeles Times* disclosed, "mean that the school will use Latinx and Chicanx in a lot of its official communications, such as news releases and publicity. The words also might end up being used in the naming of certain campus events" (Robbins 2018). New York University anchors the LatinX Project, which "explores and promotes U.S. Latinx art, culture and scholarship through creative and interdisciplinary programs" (https://wp.nyu.edu/latinxproject/). The University of Texas Press launched the "LatinX: The Future Is Now" interdisciplinary book series. Just a short while ago and in another academic context that pinpoints how LatinX learning is being shaped, the University of California, Riverside announced an open-rank faculty search for "Greater Mexico and U.S. Latinx Perspectives," with preference given to candidates focusing on areas of expertise including "Latinx/barrio urbanism"; "Latinx literature"; "Latinx performance, culture, and the visual arts"; and "Latinx education and equity" (chroniclevitae.com 2016).

These groupings are all provocative. The notion of LatinX urbanity is engrossing and merits a revisit. LatinX as a mode of being—as a designation of self—has been propagated by the outside. All kinds of things external to the LatinX self have now taken on that identifier: LatinX *is* LatinX because of the things encompassed by this panorama. As one approaches the world with critical LatinX eyes, in the contemporary sense of the word, one seeks precision on the term's performance. One might ask: what is a LatinX barrio?

This is not a frivolous query on LatinX syntax. Urban planners and housing activists must take up this exploration on the structuring of social reality too, for how is a LatinX barrio different than a Latina and Latino barrio? A U.S. barrio—*el barrio*—that houses so many constituents who would fall (and not) under LatinX subject positions, should be modified, for stylistic and conceptual consistency, to "barriX." A LatinX space may demand, as philosopher Henri Lefebvre prods, "x-dimensional spaces [. . .] spaces of configuration, abstract spaces, spaces defined by deformation and transformation" (1992, 2). A LatinX barriX is, as Lefebvre may put it, "a space of spaces" with different cultural systems that are not collapsible to Latino/a embodiment. Such a crowded, transitory barriX is a harbinger of numerous Latins and incomputable Xs.

Think back to art historian Fredo Rivera's outline of Miami as a global city and as a site of a layered LatinX pastiche where evolving urban realities lack a singular referent. Miami is an assemblage resting at the continental United States' edge. It is coevally Latin American, Caribbean, and LatinX. But LatinX "does not reflect on an identity." It connotes a more generalized Latin assortment that is cobbled together—or "a more spectacular proclamation"—of a Latinidad existing "at the scale of the global city and new media. The X is an exclamation indicative of the excess, exceptionalism, and eccentricity that constitute Miami as a port city, a globally lauded touristic haven, and a cultural and economic powerhouse" (Rivera 2019, 63). There are no fixed Latin boundaries under Rivera's purview, just LatinX immersion, in bits and pieces, where the inclusion of Haitians as LatinX is integral to Miami's transformative LatinXness.

The phases and spaces of LatinX urbanity weave together—in performance studies scholar Alexandra T. Vazquez's phraseology—a "mezclapolis," a sonic landscape with "mega mixxxxxes" (2016, 111). Vazquez devices five lowercase and lingering x's, as each one imitates, echoes, and intensifies the other, not unlike an intense assembly of dispersed and unavoidable LatinX urbanities. Different self-imaginings dissolve and are put together again in this mixxxxx-and-match (or, mixxxxx-and-patch). Ways of living and being alive are invigorated: Xs are activated through sensorial experiences, chaotic sounds, wandering melodies, and visuals. These mega mixxxxxes have "a way of subverting narrow tales of genres—of creating the new sounds it needs for itself and for us" (117). A sensory experience behind a LatinX sound may not come clearly and meticulously in "Latin."

Groundbreaking singer, actor, and supermodel Grace Jones, for instance, concretizes this LatinX mode of being in any barriX— meaning, urbanities in the world at large. The Jamaican-born iconic artist admits in *I'll Never Write My Memoirs* that she had "studied to be a Spanish teacher," and so she "had the Latin already" (2015, 115). Likewise, this observation imparts that Jones is already Latin, especially when she acknowledges that "I live in four or five time zones simultaneously, and I have four or five accents blended into one, a kind of French-Scandi-Latin-Jamerican"

(341). If Jones's case is extravagant, let's pore over her reflection on the characteristics and kinds of groups that make a barriX possible. Jones comments that it is "the nobodies, the real damaged weirdoes, obscure hipsters, gay, blacks, Latinos" that shape "the city itself" due to its "erratic, heady energy" (95).

The widespread mention of—and yearning for—"LatinX food" is another example of the seemingly coherent transference of the politics and social behavior of the "real world" to cookery and nutrition. If we return to Huerta's richly symbolic assertion of LatinX's laxativeness, the consumption of LatinX food by the LatinX body becomes less appealing. LatinX *is* what it says it eats. But what, once again, is LatinX food? How do sounds, smell, taste, inspiration, rebelliousness, and pleasure fit in the longing of a particular kind of LatinX gastronomic package that, in all probability, may alter and break the traditional mold of abuelita's "true" recipes? What are the main dishes that give this cuisine its "Latin" and "X" character as well as thrilling flavors?

Renowned Mexican chef Enrique Olvera proffers some insights on how "food is a way of communicating," in his case, the Mesoamerican nation's "old and mystical foodways and techniques, its unknown flavors, its seductive botanical diversity" (Adler 2015). I do not advocate edible excess, elaborate food adventures, or fine-dining affairs. I am trying to get a sense of the textures of how Latin taste is being adjusted in movement, not unlike the amorphous LatinX body. Consider Argentine American Korean photographer Michael Vince Kim's project chronicling Korean Mexican communities who relocated to this nation dating back to 1905 when Korea was under Japanese rule. Kim shows that one of the most memorable cultural elements is that Korean Mexicans have retained kimchi, altering their recipes to use local ingredients and gravitating toward Korean Yucatecan cultural and ethnic identifications (Gear 2017).

And give attention to Guatemalan American feinschmecker and North Carolina resident Sandra Gutierrez, who has given form to "Latin foodways, a tradition with twenty-one different cuisines" in the U.S. Southeast (2016). This heterogeneity has opened an array of opportunities for the author of *The New Southern Latino Table*. Gutierrez dubs her fusion the "New Southern-Latino Movement," an homage to a new regional way of life. Her recipes, Gutierrez states, are "happening naturally and by chance. Southerners and Latinos share similar culinary histories, ingredients, and cooking techniques, but we interpret them in very different ways. I find it exciting that, having found themselves in the same territory, these culinary traditions are correlating and intermingling" (The University of North Carolina Press 2011). Are "we" ready to embrace unrestricted LatinX creativity on a plate, going beyond dyads of authenticity and inauthenticity? Just as individuals of all ages "are reimagining their identities on platforms like Tumblr and Instagram [via] hashtags for Salvadoreñx, Argentinx, and Colombianx," will emendations be made to "our" food and eating vocabulary: arepX, arrXs con habichuelXs, biscochX, buñuelXs, chicharrXn, gazpachX, mofongX, plátanXs, picX de gallX, pupusXs, quinoX, tacXs, tortillXs, and so on (Rivas 2017)?

Google suggest—or, autocomplete—shows that curious minds are surfing and tracking LatinX's comings and goings. Precisely or imprecisely, its predictions reveal and rank information about Latinas and Latinos. They point to preoccupations about the world that are ostensibly giving cohesion to LatinX being. The internet search engine exhibits LatinX's temporal qualities and transitions. From practical questions such as "what is Latinx plural" and "why are people using [it]" to how this logic extends to other ethnoracial groups—"what is Chicanx"—these public keystrokes are crammed with many Xs shaping LatinX's story online.

The vexed concern of Latina portrayals—"what is the meaning of Latin girl," as Google indicates—is still hanging around. As is well known, the pantheon of this erotic, made-in-Hollywood Latin tradition is traced to Italian American actor and sex symbol Rudolph Valentino (1895–1926). The female counterpart to this Latin twinning includes having a racialized and promiscuous sexuality and a hot-blooded disposition, as well as being a spitfire or a tittupping figure like the Portuguese-born Brazilian performer Carmen Miranda (1909–1955). Her current millennial representation is actualized through Sofia Vergara's impersonation of Gloria Delgado-Pritchett—a curvy trophy wife with a heavy accent whose televised biography scripts an underdeveloped and rural Colombia as her homeland—in the hit ABC sitcom *Modern Family*. Vergara and Delgado-Pritchett coalesce into one Latin body. A segment of the 2017 Golden Globes Awards ceremony had the actor—the highest paid television performer five years running—pretend "her accent prevented her from being able to pronounce the word 'annual'" (Butler 2017). The words "anal" and "anus" were enunciated instead. In this sense, a "Latin girl"—a recurring *LatinX girl*, let us say somewhat incompatibly—becomes, in a manner of speaking, the "X-rated material" that gives LatinX an urgency around groupings that evoke degrees of uncontrolled pleasure and explicitness.

Latin, needless to add, has a vast and porous genealogy, extending long before the United States existed as a nation, or Spain claimed the Hispanic borderlands as part of its empire. Latin has culturally and ethnoracially jelled to Latina and Latino bodies in the American hemisphere, largely in stereotypical ways that collapse these subjects as foreign and exotic within the U.S. landscape. Renowned scholar Américo Paredes sketched "little Latins" in *George Washington Gómez: A Mexicotexan Novel* to highlight assimilatory struggles by Mexican Americans in Texas and the Southwest, a terrain that was annexed during western expansion and the 1846–1848 U.S.–Mexican War (1989). This war's final stage brought a formal agreement, the 1848 Treaty of Guadalupe Hidalgo, legally incorporating Mexicans who lived in the present-day states of Arizona, California, Colorado, Nevada, New Mexico, Texas, and Utah into the United States.

Despite their U.S. citizenship, Mexicans became a conquered population through a new racial and class structural order. The "Mexicotexan" rubric captures the unhyphenated quiddity of national and regional subjectivity straddling monumental American history. Paredes's category for Latin Americans—abridged to "little Latins" or "little things"—illustrates "a polite term" that conceals the violence of a pejorative lexicology uniting skin color with animal fat and fatty oils, as is the case with "Greaser," or a racialized nationality like "Mexican" (149, 118). Under Paredes's pen, "little Latins," inured to U.S. racism since elementary school, learn English. But they invariably think as Americans, in English, despite feeling "infinitely dirty" (148–49). Dirt can be read as the grimy substance, or as the matter that matters in the historical narration of a people who have been scaled down to a Latinness-cum-Mexicanness presumably voicing its abjection in a "Latin" tongue (see Milian 2016). It is so "Latin" and "out there," outside the "new" Texas, it might as well be LatinX.

This analytic ambiguity and fluctuation of the Latin and otherwise—a slippery Latin/X—pushes us to continually rework our tools of engagement with these categories. The letter X, as the *Oxford English Dictionary* enumerates it, is "the twenty-fourth letter of the modern and the twenty-first of the ancient Roman alphabet. [. . .] X was adopted by the Latins with the value /ks/ from the Greek alphabet introduced into Italy." The value of LatinX, as it were, is X-squared, or Latin Latin. Put another way: Latin = X and X = Latin. Yet we somehow end up at square one, as both the Latin and the X remain indeterminable: What is Latin? And what is X?

An account of LatinX warrants a frame for all the other objects, like the phalanx of material cultural items mentioned earlier that arrange and give other forms of "kinship" to Latins and their environments. If, as actor John Leguizamo has expressed, the Latinness conjured up by Tinseltown has offered "a parody of bad, flashy Latin taste," especially when it is given concrete form through a "really oily Latin accent," the material world of the LatinX takes us to another level of mass consumption and the presence of objects advancing Latin "personhood" (2007, 53). To search for LatinX––to find meaning in LatinX––we have to step into, as sociocultural anthropologist Arjun Appadurai has signaled, "the social life of things" (1988). Such an approach takes into consideration all things that are tagged with "X": who's buying; who's keying into and using the X; and how do X things speak for "us"?

X is limitless. X can be whatever it wants to be. How far can we stretch it?

The X of the Latin, The X of Our Lives

LatinX takes us to the Xs of the Latin and what they are hauling with them. What kind of X am I—as in: Central AmericanX-AmericanX (consult Arias 2003; Arias and Milian 2013)? The X is unconventional. The X is multiplying. The X is complicated. The X is funky. I like the X. I don't like the X. I loathe sounding so namby-pamby.

For the time being, I want to give thought to how we may keep pace with LatinX, how it emerges, and its interpretive routes. To get to the long and short of the hermeneutic matter: how is LatinX speaking X? LatinX pops up, in part, through hypercommodification in transnational markets as well as through the quest for intimacy. Allow me to peruse two vignettes. The first is about family ties. This kinship is the product of nonheteronormative arrangements relying on biological links that remain anonymous. The second sketch is about anonymity, discovery, and leaving some kind of imprint, however elusive. Taken together, these installments are about coming to terms with reconfigurations of the self that afford an exploration of a LatinXness of the moment.

In the spring of 2013, Mikayla Stern-Ellis, from San Diego, surfed the Tulane University website in search of a suitable college roommate. Stern-Ellis stumbled upon another Californian, Emily Nappi of San Francisco, who "had a similar build and long, wavy brown hair, just like she did." They "both also had lesbian parents and were passionate about theater." Considering the similarities and compatibilities, Stern-Ellis queried Nappi about rooming together. But Nappi had already signed up with someone else. They went on to become Facebook friends, with Stern-Ellis posting an autobiographical social media revelation on Father's Day: "Thank you Colombian sperm donor, for one of my X chromosomes." Nappi found it "odd," as she, too, had parents who had selected an unnamed Colombian sperm donor. Once at Tulane, the coincidences kept stacking up (including sleep talking and sleepwalking), until voilà, they discovered they shared the same four-digit sperm-donor numbers. They are, in a word, half-sisters (Reckdahl 2004).

The Tulane undergraduates detail their parents' motivations for in vitro fertilization (IVF) in this manner: Nappi "said her mother, a scientist, chose the 19-year-old Colombian sperm donor because he was handsome, tall, smart, athletic—he played tennis—and because he was interested in ecology, saying he wanted to save the world from global warming" (Reckdahl 2014). Stern-Ellis's parents selected this South American donor "for most of the same reasons, though his Colombian heritage was especially appealing to her because she has very light skin and thought it would be nice if her child didn't have to slather on an entire bottle of sunscreen every time she headed outside." Theirs is an undisclosed donor—a "Colombian X," so to speak—from California Cryobank, which is "known for its stringent selection process and its highly educated, young donors" (Reckdahl 2014). Since the 1970s, California Cryobank has helped create an estimated 40,000 to 50,000 babies. Stern-Ellis's mother relayed to a newspaper that this finding "is just one of the many amazing gifts" her daughter has "gotten from going to Tulane already" (Manz 2014).

To put it less formally, there's a lot going on in this story. We encounter gay family units, their rights for procreation, and the emergence of a technology a few years prior to the Reagan–Bush era's emphasis on family values and traditional mores. IVF evinces a "rapid evolution into established forms of parenthood" (Franklin 2013, 33). And, one should add, this IVF moment sheds some insights on desire through what becomes erotic Latin—or, LatinX—sperm. Concerns about environmental degradation simultaneously spring up vis-à-vis an embryonic LatinXness located in New Orleans, site of the city's catastrophic 2005 flooding by

Hurricane Katrina. This tropical cyclone foreshadows the long-term impacts that are coming in a warmer world. Not only this, but the reproductive quest for a different skin color also turns up through a longing for biologically untanned brownish skin. Facebook's online social environment makes an appearance for the Tulane millennials as well. But for the half-sisters, this conduit exceeded random content, as it led to a larger mutually constituted reality facilitated by digital consumer technology.

A précis of this fateful event: a nascent LatinXness acts out a shared affect (the two siblings, as noted, sleep talk and sleepwalk) in a geography Kirsten Silva Gruesz frames as "the 'Latinness' of New Orleans." This port city, with its British, French, Spanish, and American influences, is in a "liminal zone between the Anglo and the Latin worlds" (2006, 469). The LatinXness of these two women is manifested through affect. It resonates with how Latin is arranged in sensorial terms. Think of how aural Latinness shapes popular music discourses and consumption. The Latin Grammy Awards is a prototype where particular sounds, forms of expression, and performers amalgamate into "Latin" acts, "Latin" rhythms, and a generic "Latin" genre. The inherited Colombian Latinness of the two women—the fragments and traces of their "Latin" personality—acts out its somnambulism, a LatinXness that has yet to "fully" come into view and assume a representative pattern for a Latina and Latino "collectivity."

I do not know how these half-sisters choose to politically claim their Colombianness (or ColombianXness), and by extension, what is their general take on LatinXness. The sisters announced on their Facebook Fan Page in 2015 that they found another sibling, a brother named Greg from Fresno, California. Their post almost conveyed excitement in the unknown and in waiting for future family members. This case broadly highlights what I am attempting to disentangle: the politics of Latina and Latino bodies, the cobbling together of ethnoracial identity, the anticipation of the loose memberships that inform it, and the narratives of the corporeal and conceptual passing into a flux of LatinXness.

Notions of Latin completeness come undone through Rafael Antonio Lozano Jr., a computer programmer who majored in philosophy at the University of Texas at Austin and goes by the sobriquet "Winter." The subject of the 2006 documentary *Starbucking*, Winter's raison d'être has been, since 1997, to visit every Starbucks in the world. The objective of his "Starbucks Everywhere" project is to patronize five to twenty shops on a given day and sample coffee from each location.

Winter concedes that he does not promote the colossal Seattle-based company. Yet his gobbling up of Starbucks-branded caffeine yokes him to the unevenly developed coffee-producing nations that blend with the U.S. Latin. Return to another inveterate figure of Latinness—a "Columbianness" constituted over time—through the iconic Juan Valdez, the mythical coffee picker and brand character made up by the National Federation of Coffee Growers of Colombia in 1958. As journalist Juan Forero abridged it in the *New York Times*, Valdez is "one of advertising's most successful fictional characters—the mustachioed farmer, a poncho over his shoulder and [a] trusty mule" named Conchita at his side, helping "make Colombian coffee world famous" (2001). Becoming a "gentle and wholesome rural symbol," in geographer Ian Maclachlan's words, Valdez, represented and certified "100% Colombian Coffee" (2012, 407). Winter—who is paying great homage to the Global North's cold season without much reverence for the "natural" ambiance attributed to the "tropical" Latin—uses coffee as another articulation of allegiance and cultural belonging.

Just as memoirist and novelist Brando Skyhorse acknowledges that even though his mother "had been born to Mexican parents, she spoke—and would learn—nothing beyond fast-food Spanish," Winter, too, hints at how the linguistically "luxurious" Latin becomes manifest by expressing the "instant" pleasures of the senses acquired through the emergent environments of the new American "home" (2014, 22). The excess that shapes "all-American meals" informs this junk food Spanish, an ordinary and omnipresent vernacular. Its stylized repetition may be scanty, limited, and occasionally tripped up, but it improvises and communicates the Latin's trajectory. Winter's "coffeehouse Spanish" is an outlet to how Latins, as "common" but indefinable people, operate in the world. The frequency of their jargon—regular; extra shot; "skinny" latte; light roast/dark roast; single-origin; sugar/no sugar; extra hot—insinuates how a Latin "supply" is permutated, a residual X that may break the mood or muddle up the conversation, for they are expressing the (Latin) inexpressible and its characterization of an un-American life. The coffeehouse yields a different way of being "at home," a social life that can be the "same," if you will, anywhere.

Winter told a Delaware newscast that Starbucks Everywhere was "a random idea that popped into my mind, while I was at a Starbucks talking about how quickly this company was growing. Everywhere you turned, there'd be a new store in the Dallas area, and I thought, 'What if I could visit them all? And what if I could be the only person?' So about a year later, I hit the road, and I just fell in love with the process. I mean, just driving cross-country, trying to find these places, which is sometimes easier said than done, meeting new people, getting to see things that I'd never seen before. [. . .] The thing is they keep building stores, [. . .] so it's a never-ending quest" (YouTube 2007). The brown subject—or, pardon the unavoidable pun, the coffee-colored Winter—expands the self through corporate growth, frequenting, at last count, 15,077 Starbucks in the United States and Canada and 3,139 stores in Europe, Asia, and the Middle East (Winter n.d.). Latinoness is intangible, as Winter casts light on "something"—coffee, the crop, and the commodity—that is "singularly unique" to him. He stands apart from the business people, the professors, and the crowds who walk in and out of their daily routines. Just as coffee can be ubiquitous, so can the Latin with its mixxxxxtures.

Since 2012, Winter has revamped his mission with the task he now dubs as "Anywhere but Starbucks." His everywhere and anywhere venture captures a restless energy by being connected to—and "reformatted" by—an elsewhere: "hot spots" of unclear,

LatinX genealogies tinkered with along the way. His LatinXness is experienced through deleterious affect—nausea, stomach pain, and hyperactivity due to his constant hits of caffeine—a Latin spectacle walking alongside the locations of Latinas and Latinos in popular imaginations. Winter embodies a new site: he is a localized "foreign" import.

In the realm of the popular culture canon, Winter—our rather "strange" Winter, or, by now, our rather familiar stranger, making a name for himself, making noise in the world—may be deemed as unserious, forgettable, even "trash" reality TV material. But what are the aesthetics of LatinX, and should its cultural ranges always be of "great quality"? What attracts and demands my involvement, alas, are the snapshots of the "fake" and/or improper comings and goings of the Latin and the "public" personality that may be attributed to it. Which is to say that X is a series of ongoing differences. The coffeehouse facilitates these ersatz and fidgety performances of Winter's being—a "foreignness" in origin that is infallibly "here." Winter epitomizes questions about new ways of consumption and communication, paired with the supplemental identifications of LatinXs, which move away from recognizable modes of Latinoness and Latinaness. Can we catch up to Winter's deracinated and unpredictable LatinXness on a global scale?

Sincerely Yours, XOXO

The life of X is passing through the realities of our American and Latin lives. I have taken this occasion to investigate and insist that there's mandatory work to be done with the plexus of entangled Xs being passed around. Xs are not a single body of ethnoracial, cultural, or gendered identification, but an expressive and communicative semiotic with an array of participants and observers.

In ending with the epistolary rhetorical practice of signing one's name with the parting phrase "sincerely yours," I am, in a way, reimagining the "rules" of correspondence. I present a different "agreement." It is an ending and an opening. It is, sincerely, an attempt to bring to life the friend, the reader, and the critic as a set of individuals, an evolving political family, an unassigned bounty of Xs.

The X can be ordinary. The X can be rich. Kaleidoscopic. Transplantable. The X is flourishing, present, and living. Will you pass it up, or pass it on?

Forms

LOOKING AT THE BOTTOM of the Central American map, attempting to look up—to Mexico, to the United States, and to the plurality of borders people cross, defying the illusion that there's only one physical border, the Mexico–U.S. border—I turn to the spectacular production and "documentation" of the LatinX child migrant. One of LatinX's potent features is that it captures the emergence of uprooted subjects thrown into an unexpected array of circumstances.

I reflect on Valeria Luiselli's creative nonfiction undertaking, *Tell Me How It Ends: An Essay in Forty Questions* (2017). This work by the widely acclaimed Mexican novelist is "a deceptively slim volume," to give an aperçu of National Public Radio's view (Powers 2017). Luiselli's account moves with an eye toward what became known, as a Wikipedia entry enumerates it, the "2014 American immigration crisis" (Wikipedia n.d.). This uncertain moment in American life refers to the influx into the United States of unaccompanied minors from Central America's Northern Triangle—El Salvador, Guatemala, and Honduras—or "the most murderous corner of the world," as renowned Salvadoran journalist Óscar Martínez describes it (2016, xviii). Their reasons for fleeing cannot be easily shrugged off: the children are escaping "extreme violence, persecution and coercion by gangs, mental and physical abuse, forced labor, neglect, abandonment" (12). The unauthorized entries were expected to reach seventy thousand in 2014 alone, an outpouring that led President Barack Obama to declare it a "humanitarian crisis" (Gordon 2014).

Luiselli enters this course of events as a volunteer interpreter for a New York City federal immigration court. "My task there

is a simple one," she explains. "I interview children in court, following the intake questionnaire, and then translate their stories
from Spanish to English" (2017, 7). Her main subject, Central
American child migrants striving to exist (to say nothing of their
presupposed questionable motivations for defying their national
origins—for not sticking to their moira—and illegally coming to
the United States) deepens the urgency of Luiselli's work. Their
stories are activated by a standardized American questionnaire—a
mechanical list of unyielding items following a template, moving
from one child to the ostensible monotonous sameness of the next
one's responses. The sum of the questionnaire's forty parts presumably tells us all we need to know (40). But a different history is
burgeoning through these all-too-familiar Central American children, their life-and-death circumstances, and the way things work
in the courtroom. Luiselli's approach revitalizes the immigration
questionnaire's purpose by attenuating its routineness with a fo-
cus on the uniqueness of the responses.

Luiselli and the child migrant navigate a document in the service of national security, the rule of law, and public welfare. The
questionnaire—a preliminary standardized American test—is a
tool that measures, that now and then lets in but that ultimately deports, time and again, the unauthorized migrant. The book's forty
questions invite an analysis of the function of its very framework—
the questions—as the Central American child is actualized in the
public sphere through this test. How, we must ask, is the Central
American children's humanity attended to via contemporary bureaucratic U.S. documentation? Readers are compelled to engage
with the document to see a kind of Central American abject humanity, which is part of the problem. The questionnaire is a catalyst—a portal to enter the discussion of the U.S. Central American
presence through the minor. It is foundational to our understanding of the becoming of the Central American "thing," the unaccompanied minor, in the United States.

But what is the questionnaire actually doing? How are Central
American children made into the word on bureaucratic paper? My

efforts attempt to create a language beyond the paper, so that the emergence of the problem child is understood.

The questionnaire—a file of information and personal experience—demonstrates a genealogy of temporary American beginnings. *Tell Me How It Ends* is a bid to "tell me how *you* begin"—how the outré LatinX child is configured within juridical archival projects, within American rhetoric and practice, and within the historical space that does not admit Latina and Latino bodies. It is the U.S. questionnaire—not the passport—that operates as a nexus of organizational attention, indicating the Central American child's unauthorized entry and providing a nebulous "history of the documentation of individual identity" (Robertson 2010, 3). This form—as sociologist John Torpey speculates in connection to "the invention of the passport"—makes "their relevant differences knowable and thus enforceable," maintaining "documentary control" on their movement (2000, 2–3). The questionnaire grants an identity that confers restricted access to American spaces, but through a matter where the why of this minor arises. Luiselli gives insight into how the child migrant interacts with perhaps one of the most contentious and tangled questions of our contemporary moment: "Why did you come to the United States?" (2017, 7). The why—*their* why—discloses a Central American sociopolitical reality that does not placate the public and limits the minor's being in the American world.

If, as philosopher Thomas Nail advances, the twenty-first century is "the century of the migrant," our epoch, too, is globally marked, in large scale, by the *child* migrant (2015, 1). "Migration to developed states" by children and young people under twenty, affirms public policy scholar Jacqueline Bhabha, "has more than doubled in the last thirty-five years." In cases when migrant children "did not have families to care for them," they "became the responsibility of diasporic community organizations from their countries of origin—Ethiopia, Iran, Vietnam, Somalia, Sri Lanka, El Salvador, Guatemala. Formal legal decisions were not taken on their behalf, and state entities did not take responsibility for their well-being" (2016, 2). Recall 2016 headlines that stressed the absence of protective attention for unaccompanied minors migrating to Europe. Thousands of moving children from Syria, Afghanistan, or Eritrea are missing or have been "accommodated" to the needs of the dark and intricate infrastructures of Greece's and Italy's informal marketplaces. A BBC title inquired, "Why Are 10,000 Migrant Children Missing in Europe?" The answer is disturbing: smugglers may be "turning the children they bring into Europe into the hands of traffickers to make more money. Those children might then be pushed into prostitution or slavery" (Merriman 2016). These migration patterns, routes of power, and forces of exploitation moving along with unaccompanied minors warrant studies from various researchers and experts in numerous fields and across geographies.

This juncture also merits new questions on mobility, the presence of children, and their restrictive U.S. contexts alongside the everyday spaces of their lives. Transnational migrations, generally an adult-centered topic, are understood through assimilation, hyphenation, remittances, or full subjectivities. The "unaccompanied alien child," as the legal term construes them, navigates a number of worlds with—as the Mesoamerican corridor evinces—underworlds invariably lurking nearby. Central American minors—their agency, discoveries, and evolving stories—are fertilizing the field as well as the intellectual reach of Latino/a studies and its unlikely spaces in the Global South.

But there is no final intellectual destination. How do the courses of these minors' mobility—their livelihood, the tensions, their different embodiments, and the imprints they leave behind in movement, in detention, in U.S. life, and in deportation processes—readjust the discursive edifice not so much of Latino/a ontological being but of deracinated emergence? By deracination I mean more than location or national uprootedness. It is a possibility to think about fragmentation, dissemination, and reconfiguration—an ungroundedness that decouples geographic fundamentality, specificity, and essentialism from the meaning of Latina and Latino in the United States. Latino/a is never fully situated in the world.

The LatinX child's trajectory lends a hand in how these concerns with unpredictable starting points are disentangled.

Zigzagging our way through these conceptual thickets requires a brief explanation about the titular adjective moving this critical itinerary forward: LatinX. This gender-neutral denomination, to quickly review and summarize this term's fundamentals, is deemed the current alternative to U.S. Latina and Latino ethnoracial labels. LatinX—predominantly employed by scholars, activists, artists, and journalists—substitutes the terminological ilk of Latina/o, Latino/a, and Latin@. Online news outlets such as ColorLines, Fusion, *Huffington Post*, *Latina*, and Latino USA have been among the first to elucidate LatinX's meaning (see Logue 2015; Funes 2017; Latino USA 2016; Reichard 2016; Rivas 2017). LatinX "first began to emerge within queer communities on the Internet in 2004." It makes room "for people who are trans, queer, agender, non-binary, gender non-conforming or gender fluid," as the X rejects "the gendering of words especially since Spanish is such a gendered language" (Ramirez and Blay 2016).

I do not quarrel about, or submit, "correct" definitions. What attracts me about LatinX is its range of possibilities, its myriad pathways, and its wilting of conformity. The LatinX rhetorical gesture, as a matter of orientation in thought, is a ponderable one for our intellectual generation (see Chandler 2013). LatinX is more than just about Spanish as a gendered Romance language. The X is unknowable—or beyond knowing. The classification itself, LatinX, remains unknown, which is to say that we have rendered ourselves to the unknown—or the unknowns of unpredictable worlds. In this regard, LatinX can critically and imaginatively operate as "a guide to getting lost," to extract from essayist Rebecca Solnit, wherein we—quite riveted and wide awake—"leave the door open for the unknown, the door into the dark. That's where the most important things come from, where you yourself came from, and where you will go" (2005, 4).

The Latin and the X are marked by, and prolong in, indeterminacy. Latin and X are capitalized to put their discursive functioning and communicative tensions in analytic play and to highlight how these dual-directional signifiers elicit continuous discernment. I steer toward LatinX in the context of unaccompanied Central American minors thrown into urgency, migration, detention, crises, and questionnaires: the X of our actual moment in history. The X of the LatinX child subsumes many Xs: lest we forget, there is more than one LatinX child. The scattered LatinX child lives at the margins of the unknown, of the double uncertainty of the Xs of the Latino/a world and the American one. Its centrality of being is its abject, threatening knownness. The LatinX child has been depersonalized and dehumanized, far removed from the here and now.

This scrutiny delves into the broader concept of the expulsed Central American child as a newcomer, a migrant, and the beginning of something else: a LatinX phenomenon of, and in, crisis. By beginning I mean all that starts afresh: the LatinX child's inception is characteristic of how it came into being, as literary theorist and public intellectual Edward Said put forward (1975, 174–75). His preoccupations come within the LatinX child's range, for "the notion of a beginning itself is practically tied up in a whole complex of relations. Between the word beginning and the word origin lies a constantly changing system of meanings" (5–6). Beginnings "inaugurate a deliberately *other* production of meaning": they are "a problem to be studied," "preparatory to something else" (13–14). Origins, by contrast, are passive, tied to "precedence and unchanging being," where "everything can be referred for an explanation" (174). While Central America is an origin—as in a "source," the first stage of existence, or, as Nail conjectures, the "socially fixed point *from which*" the LatinX child "departs"—I benefit from Said's cogitation on beginnings, as they do not subscribe to purity (14). Beginnings challenge a subject's simplification to a decisive origin or a point in time. They are vectors emphasizing direction, sharing a spirit of possibilities-cum-possible disappointments. Provisional beginnings—chosen beginnings, geographic beginnings, murky beginnings—as novelist Edwidge Danticat (2019) has observed, "have a much bigger burden and are often less clear."

This LatinX beginning—beginning of something else—requires that we wrestle, on and on, as Said makes clear, with "the tumbling disorder that will not settle down" for Latins looming under that capacious and changeable X (50). The LatinX child advancing these pages begins through the Mesoamerican journey, at odds with the American child's safe domestic movements. Reflecting on childhood wanderings, getting lost, and its activation of the creative imagination, Solnit writes: "Children seldom roam, even in the safest places. Because of their parents' fear of the monstrous things that might happen (and do happen, but rarely), the wonderful things that happen as a matter of course are stripped away from them. For me, childhood roaming was what developed self-reliance, a sense of direction and adventure, imagination, a will to explore, to be able to get a little lost and then figure out the way back" (2005, 7). What does the LatinX child imaginatively conjure up during movement or "adventure"? Unaccompanied minors turn themselves over to the Border Patrol, to American bureaucracy, upon making it to the other side. There is a certain innocence in Solnit's passage. But the questionnaire's LatinX child is already inscribed into a transcriptional practice. Which is to say that we need another beginning to Luiselli's end. For the LatinX child, "roaming" is at odds with their journey. The LatinX child locomotes with motivation and will. The LatinX traveler is still a child and still unable to move through the bureaucracy of their final destination.

Anthropologist Susan J. Terrio sets forth that "when the number of unaccompanied children crossing the US–Mexico border from October 2013 to June 2014 surged to 57,525, moral panic centered on the threat of criminality and disease they posed" (2015, 10). The reader, thrust into Luiselli's text vis-à-vis an exigent crisis, learns how movement and detention inaugurate—indeed, usher along—the LatinX child, or the ex-child who does not quite fall back to childhood. Let us consider, too, that there is another X-child in Luiselli's enterprise: her unnamed five-year-old daughter, a key questioner who often asks her, "So, how does the story of those children end?" (2017, 55). Through her child's eye—another witness account—we see an unbreakable feedback between mother and daughter. Luiselli's titular intent could just as readily be amended to *(You) Tell Me How It Ends (Mamá)*, or even *(You) Tell Me How It Ends (Mamá, Because It's Different from How Your Story Ended)*. The Central American minor is perhaps the most X of the children that are "out there." What is LatinX in relation to child migrants? What is a LatinX life, given its dissonances, incoherence, and fluctuating borders? How are their LatinXness *and* AmericanXness put into words? I pursue these concerns through an unfolding LatinXness underpinned by notions of nascency. Like the Central American child, this incipience is intangible, deracinated, aspirational, and far from unified—transcending "the nation" and struggling to "make sense."

Tell Me How It Ends obliges readers to sift through historical antecedents of the questionnaire and its circulations to try to find a working order of the racialized Central American child in it. I start by drawing on a brief overview of surveys and the narratives they have proffered to the nation as well as its citizens— illustrating, during these beginning moments of Central American inscription, that "the future is only the stuff of some kids," as performance studies theorist José Esteban Muñoz made known (2009, 95). From there, I interrogate the meanings of U.S. crisis in Central American life.

The Central American Minor / The Minor Central American

Migration from Central America to the United States is not a recent occurrence. Sociologist Norma Stoltz Chinchilla and political scientist Nora Hamilton note that the isthmus's civil wars during the 1980s—in conjunction with "the effects of Hurricane Mitch and other natural disasters in the 1990s, and deteriorating economic conditions, as well as a demand for immigrant labor in certain U.S. labor markets"—set in motion their steady migratory flows (2007, 328). Since "a substantial number of Central American immigrants are undocumented," they add, this "constitutes an important obstacle to their economic success, limiting the kinds of jobs available to them and resulting in frequent exploitation of their labor. In contrast to Cubans and Vietnamese, Salvadorans, Guatemalans, and Nicaraguans were not accepted as refugees during the 1980s, and very few were able to obtain asylum" (333).

Sociologist Pierrette Hondagneu-Sotelo underscores that "Salvadoran and Guatemalan women and men left their countries in haste, often leaving their children behind, as they fled the civil wars, political violence, and upheaval" (2007, 53). Journalistic endeavors such as Sonia Nazario's *Enrique's Journey* (2007)—originally a six-part *Los Angeles Times* series from 2002, which earned the Pulitzer Prize for Feature Writing—looked into the psychological impact of gendered migrations on Central American families. Nazario chronicled how Enrique, a teenager, traveled alone from Honduras to search for his mother in the United States, feeling, as some Central American children frequently do, abandoned. Central American children are not, clearly, the first or the last to take a questionnaire. Yet the survey—how it ideologically strengthens itself and keeps tabs on the unwanted migrant child—gives "birth" to expellable intruders who are seen precisely because of their "illegality" and Central Americanness. The questionnaire is a legitimate form that makes these undocumented subjects speak and legible to a social order. Central American children are foregrounded as nomadic and oral—at odds with the written records structuring the nation and its families.

Historian Sarah Igo imparts that "the promise of empirical surveys," with its prying inquisitiveness, is "to disclose the society to itself" (2007, 2). Mass surveys entered the public domain after World War I, "telling Americans 'who we are,' 'what we want,' and 'what we believe'" (3). Doubtlessly, there are "many other ways to envision America, beginning with works of literature, photography, and history" (4). "Americans today," Igo proceeds, "are accustomed to a seemingly endless stream of questions from survey researchers, political pollsters, marketers, and census takers.

Being studied, and being privy to the results, is an understood and unexceptional feature of modern life. It is perhaps the principal way that we know ourselves to be a part of the national community" (2–3). Contemporary U.S. life is inundated with countless types of questionnaires shared on social media. Personality tests, dating profiles, and "our obsession with online quizzes" manifest "a nonstop, exhausting performance" of selfhood (Maloney 2014). MIT psychologist and cultural analyst Sherry Turkle emphasizes that the quizzes' function "is to share it, to feel 'who you are' by how you share who you are" (Maloney).

This globally networked relationality—or untiring "linking" of the technological self that is always *on*—involves an active makeover that recurrently performs and reveals a new kind of temporal life. But this reworking of the self cannot be neatly connected to unsummoned, unaccompanied Central American children and the "confessional" responses required in off-line questionnaires for U.S. courtrooms. "As you make your way down its forty questions," Luiselli avers, "it's impossible not to feel that the world has become a much more fucked-up place than anyone could have ever imagined" (2017, 10). These children's stigmatized bodies are a mismatch. They cannot, on the face of it, afford quality things and habitually tinker with the self through smart technological gadgets. Unable to readily catch up to the ongoing, updated reinvention encountered online, they come across as distant from the everyday American. And the questionnaire, as applied to administered Central Americans in U.S. courtrooms, upholds the value of American organizational life, of an efficient American bureaucracy that competently deports them. The disruption is not the procedural paper logic that writes them off, or the history of American intervention that has produced these displacements. The Central American minor is disruption embodied.

But I want to follow, for a bit, the historical thread of the questionnaire and its associations to notions of geography, pedigree, racial hierarchies, and moral characteristics. Evan Kindley's *Questionnaire* (2016) keeps a finger on the pulse of nineteenth-century efforts to draft surveys envisioning "a world remade by asking the right questions" (11). Another way to put it may be that the "right" questions asked by the "right" kind of people led to a "righted" world, as English explorer and anthropologist Francis Galton intended. A cousin of Charles Darwin, Galton coined the scientific and social movement known as eugenics in 1883 and is recognized for this form's early and meticulous uses. He designed questionnaires promoting the development of the sciences of anthropometrics, statistics, and evolutionary biology. Galton's surveys—"scientific investigations"—were fortuitous. Parents became "family historians," preserving a "trustworthy record" of their "biological experience" through their children (Galton 1884). These family catalogs gave rise to "the baby book, a popular genre that continues to flourish today" (Kindley 2016, 14).

Galton's investment in purity, development, and fitness from infancy onward coincided with the extreme representation, during England's Victorian age (1837–1901), of Máximo and Bartola, two "diminutive, primary microcephalic" Central American siblings. Known for their "'dwarfish and idiotic' appearance," they toured both sides of the Atlantic (Bogdan 1988, 127–28). A Spanish trader approached Máximo and Bartola's parents to take them from El Salvador to the United States and cure them of their "imbecility" (128). Arguably, Máximo and Bartola are the genesis of Central American "unaccompanied minors." Later sold to an American, the brother and sister were refashioned as "Aztec children" by their owner-manager, who metamorphosed them into objects of "vivid interest" at a time when Americans "thirsted for more information about the natural history of their own continent" (128, 130).

The "Aztec Lilliputians" were guests of President Millard Fillmore at the White House and created "quite a stir" in England (Bogdan 1988, 130). They were exhibited at P. T. Barnum's American Museum in New York and before the Ethnological Society of London. Máximo and Bartola also met the royal family at Buckingham Palace. They progressed from "sensation to specimen"—having been declared "a new type of humanity, only three feet high"—as literary scholar Robert D. Aguirre reveals (2005, 105). Máximo and Bartola had been rendered, in a word, inanimate objects. They performed for their own moment in time, foreshadowing the grotesqueries of the Central American future.

This snapshot casts light on the rhetorical and processual building up of the questionnaire, especially during industrialization and during a time of change. In the 1880s the number of excluded classes in the U.S. immigration system grew, as historian Mae Ngai has discussed, "to comprise the mentally retarded, contract laborers, persons with 'dangerous and loathsome contagious disease,' paupers, polygamists, and the 'feebleminded' and 'insane,' as well as Chinese laborers" (2004, 59). Victorian scholar Sally Mitchell writes that across the Atlantic the textures of everyday life, "the physical and technological surroundings in which people lived, the patterns of their education and work and recreation and belief, were [all] utterly transformed" (1996, xiv). This transition period parallels our contemporary time, with the digitization of life. Yet the more connected we are digitally, the more disconnected we become. Sentimentality and the representation of emotions are attributed to inanimate children like Máximo and Bartola—not unlike the projected dark brownness and stillness of minors in a questionnaire.

Obsessive scientific approaches and racialized lenses are applied to "things," to "monstrous" differences that help hegemonic subjects understand their normality and superiority. But it is a "monstrosity" that must be kept afar. Terrio expounds that "terms such as *racial purity* have largely disappeared from public usage, but racial thinking is expressed in coded language about work, education, immigration, and entitlements" (2015, 9). Organizational and managerial control does not trail too far behind. Anthropologist David Graeber reminds us of this when he observes that bureaucratic procedure "invariably means ignoring all the subtleties of real human existence and reducing everything to simple pre-established mechanical or statistical formulae. Whether it's a matter of forms, rules, statistics, or questionnaires, bureaucracy is always about simplification" (2011, 51).

Luiselli attempts to limn, sardonically, America's normative fears when it comes to the child migrant from Central America—a region that, in foreign affairs journalist Tim Marshall's rendering, "has little going for it by way of geography but for one thing. It is thin" (2015, 226). Marshall posits a different relation to the area and its human subjects, a new sense of getting caught up in "that" Central American "thin(g)": that trivial thin thing. Luiselli writes:

> In varying degrees, some papers and webpages announce the arrival of undocumented children like a biblical plague. Beware the locusts! They will cover the face of the ground so that it cannot be seen— these menacing, coffee-colored boys and girls, with their obsidian hair and slant eyes. They will fall from the skies, on our cars, on our green lawns, on our heads, on our schools, on our Sundays. They will make a racket, they will bring their chaos, their sickness, their dirt, their brownness. They will cloud the pretty views, they will fill the future with bad omens, they will fill our tongues with bar- barisms. And if they are allowed to stay here they will—eventually— reproduce. (2017, 15)

To be clear: I admire Luiselli's oeuvre, her thoughtfulness, and, as she demonstrates, her readiness and skill to witness, translate, and discharge the concrete problem back to her American addressees. *Tell Me How It Ends* is a testament that the Central American mi- nor has not been kicked out of the American world so silently. Luiselli raises awareness—"a transformation of consciousness," as author Nathaniel Popkin rightly gauged in *Literary Hub* (2017)— and appeals to a U.S. goodness that will engender reason and dig- nity to Central American children.

It is almost as though the reader is privy to Luiselli's Latina becoming. She is an alien—a "nonresident alien" wanting to be- come a "resident alien"—wrestling with the green card question- naire and the unresolvable question, "Why did you come to the United States?" (2017, 8–10). I understand her intended irony in the aforementioned excerpt, a tricky thing to capture. Yet the ease of the prose—the circulation of this cultural representation—does not read as ironic. The passage sounds eerily like eugenics. To whom are these words of "disfigurement" directed? These signifiers conceivably legitimate these minors' geopolitical and racial differences—marking them as "real." Central American differences are unchangeable. Most ironically, isn't that why these minors are policed, detained, and deported in the first place?

Ultimately, what does such a passage contribute? Can we grasp "their" difference only through this repetition of saturated difference? *What* is this LatinX child's difference? The LatinX child may not be called a rapist or a predator in the U.S. lingua franca, as undocumented adults are usually dubbed. But perhaps Luiselli's double-edged comments about this political problem are unerring to the extent that the semiotics applied to the unlawful child migrant's racialized meanings are not so color-blind. This racialization is at odds with how, as constitutional scholar Patricia Williams has pointed out, U.S. children in predominantly white schools are told by "well-meaning teachers" such hackneyed expressions as, "Color makes no difference," and "It doesn't matter whether you're black or white or red or green or blue" (1997, 3). Seemingly, the LatinX child—none or all of the above—is muffled in the classroom and remains outside the colorings of this colorless palette, of this discursive elision of race. The Central American child becomes what "we" already "know" "it" is, or, as Luiselli synthesizes it, "barbarians who deserve subhuman treatment" (2017, 84).

Binding the minor to the precision of the survey's questions, we only "know" Central American children as juridical subjects, as an impure matter on which American power will be exercised. Not an American child but more like a contemptible child without discipline and with a slew of undesirable attributes, this minor treads a path far from straight and narrow. Who are they, what are their origins, and where are their parents? Luiselli explains that "the process by which a child is asked questions during the intake interview is called screening." She continues:

> Right before the first formal interview question, a line floats across the page like an uncomfortable silence:
> Where is the child's mother?___father?___

There are no family trees to reconstruct this "floating" population: only blank lines resting, "floating," on genealogical "imperfection." They surface as empty, anonymous Xs "filled" by a blank univocality unified by abandonment and unknowability. The Central American child transfigures into the LatinX child, coming to us from a different "Latin" world. Its adjacent AmericanXness is never far behind: LatinXness and AmericanXness have been birthed in crisis (Luiselli 2017, 11).

This child's relatives are nonrelatives. The LatinX child's "authenticity" is the X that looks odd, that duplicates, that is both paper and paperwork. The X of blank-headedness and bureaucratic runaround. The X of heightened exclusion. The X that requires the LatinX child to be "realistic." The X of not knowing where or how it will end up. The X that drops by. The X of stigma and confinement. The X that cannot cross out the (Northern Triangle) error. The LatinX child is resistant to closure.

"Too often, the spaces remain blank," Luiselli divulges. "All the children come without their fathers and their mothers. And many of them do not even know where their parents are" (2017, 11). These are families in crisis. Buried in a particular "grammar book," as literary theorist Hortense J. Spillers might put it, this Central American "baby"—a "notorious bastard" that is always Mama's, Papa's, and the nation's "maybe"—grows into "a resource for metaphor" (1987, 66). The absence of the mother and father for the Central American child evolves into a "territory of cultural and political maneuver" (67). Central American minors become illegitimate children with illegitimate claims. Spillers's methodological conception of U.S. historical order as it relates to black womanhood, enslavement, and African American family structures is, needless to add, distinct from migrant children who "try to turn themselves in to the migra, or Border Patrol, as soon as possible" (20). Yet I revisit Spillers's work to deliberate on this migrant "anomaly"—on Central American "faults" and "failures" from early childhood—and the new kind of "grammar," the "altered human factor," the X, produced in transit. "The migration of children," Luiselli regards with keen attention, "is reorganizing and redefining the traditional family structure" (2017, 48).

The Central American child is "unthinkable" (Luiselli 2017, 12). To trouble this pronouncement further: it is not the minor per se who is unthinkable. Central American children and their ballooning numbers are simply unthinkable *in* the United States—and extraordinarily unthinkable in the American long run. Seen as such, these minors "deserve," as Bhabha has it, punitive treatment, punitive intervention, and punitive measures that return them "to the places they fear" (2016, 207). Their predicament—and the ugliness that surrounds their plight, to say nothing of their unhealthy nations—exhibits an unfitness registering the isthmus's dangers and pathologies. LatinX children can never really speak of a *new* life, only attest to their ever-present abjection. Their "floating" explanations steadily go south—taking these minors, literally, back to Central America.

Luiselli swiftly resurrects a passage from a Reuters story in which the news agency reported that "looking happy the deported children exited the airport on an overcast and sweltering afternoon. One by one, they filed into a bus, playing with the balloons they had been given" (2017, 16). Calling this far-from-festive sight an "uncanny image," Luiselli "cannot stop reproducing" it "somewhere in the dark back of our minds." Reuters's characterization of deportation as "fun and games" is, shall we say, haunting, almost suggesting that expelled children must play—or, rather, that adult readers must be comforted by—the positive role of being happy under these circumstances. The balloon is like a goody of care, a party favor, a temporary consolation prize. The balloon and the minor are easy to puncture and deflate: deflatable goods for deflatable children. Children and balloons, both familiar in daily life, become strange and unfamiliar. They are the contents of an awkward and outrageous performance that "fits" in the culture of a detention and deportation system through a different form of "crisis management." There is no management model to improve the practice of admitting Central American children into the United States, just the coordination of detention and mass expulsions.

The LatinX child is pliable. Childhood and adulthood are on the same hostile footing. The Central American minor (as in: under the legal age of full responsibility) interchangeably becomes a minor Central American (meaning: someone who has a low rank, status, or position)—enacting an ideological Lilliputianness at the jurid-ical level. The diminutiveness of the LatinX child—a descendant of Máximo's and Bartola's, so to speak—evokes magnification: the magnification of smallness through time. Lilliputianness is a met-aphor for Central America and the Central American. The ques-tionnaire mirrors this shortness by condensing and minimizing its subject. The fantastical smallness of Máximo and Bartola makes a return as the little LatinX child is shortened through his or her questionnaire responses in our modern day. After all, immigration judge Jack H. Weil has argued that "three- and four-year-olds can learn immigration law well enough to represent themselves in court. I've taught immigration law literally to three-year-olds and four-year-olds. It takes a lot of time. It takes a lot of patience. They get it. It's not the most efficient, but it can be done" (Markon 2016).

The LatinX child is expected to possess the brainpower to figure out U.S. immigration law and to competently serve as its own legal counsel. This child acts out a legally sanctioned bizarre irrational-ism. The LatinX child stages the juridical mode of recognition by which it is identified: its abject problems. But there is no sense of American ethics and obligation to the Central American child who appears to arrive ex nihilo. Three additional judges publicly chal-lenged Weil: "A typical three-year-old cannot tie her shoes, count to 100, peel a banana, or be trusted not to swallow marbles" (Markon 2016). Luiselli mentions the cognitive stumbling blocks presented by the form's last ten questions. They "are the most difficult because they refer directly to the gangs. Smaller children look back at you with a mixture of bewilderment and amusement if you say 'bands of organized criminals,' maybe because they associate the word 'bands' with musical groups" (2017, 73). The LatinX child, "targeted on the basis of racialized national identities," is framed to articulate its own grounds of expulsion (Terrio 2015, 15). Ngai's words ring true: if "the illegal immigrant cannot be constituted without deportation—the possibility or threat of deportation, if not the fact"—neither can the LatinX child (2004, 58). Illegality, detention, and deportation are its iconic status.

One is not a detached observer. Luiselli speaks of two Guatemalan sisters, five and seven years old, whose mother saved enough money to bring them up north through a coyote or, as one of the girls says, "a man" (2017, 56). They prepared for their journey in this way:

> The day before they left, their grandmother sewed a ten-digit number on the collars of the dress each girl would wear through the entire trip. It was a ten-digit number the girls had not been able to memorize, as hard as she tried to get them to, so she had decided to embroider it on their dresses and repeat over, and over, a single instruction: they should never take this dress off, not even to sleep, and as soon as they reached America, as soon as they met the first American policeman, they were to show the inside of the dress's collar to him. He would then dial the number and let them speak to their mother. The rest would follow. (57)

Luiselli calls attention to the "ten-digit number." This incomprehensible phone number—as unknowable as XXX-XXX-XXXX—cannot be repeated memoriter. It cannot come any further than Luiselli's qualifier: the ten-digit number. At times U.S. businesses make phone numbers catchier by using letters or phrases in place of digits. But this ingenious grandmother clears this obstacle by fashioning her own system of communication. By the same token, there is no punctual sense of clock and calendar time—no one knows the length of this arduous and risky journey, just the descriptor "through the entire trip." The girls are "timed" by the number of borders they continue to cross in their coded, unchangeable dresses, a sort of borderlands uniform in this Mesoamerican space of "standard stranded time," as it were. They are "timed," as well, by their bodies—children's bodies keeping up with adult paces, a coyote's speed, moving forward—which assume, one can only speculate, a physical and psychological toll. Their grandmother tells their story of crossing boundaries through her needlework—stitching a U.S. recognizable, registered, and working number, a

"good" number, on a collar to be shown, like official documentation, to American government agents on arrival. But this dress is
a different activation of caller ID, let's say, for one cannot predict
who will access and dial the ten digits: a U.S. police officer or a
member of a gang or an organized crime group. The dress and
its discreet phone number presage life and death, good and bad
news, farness and nearness, childhood home and detention center,
crossing with fear and living with fear.

"The children that arrived here, one must remember, are also the
children that made it. The children that made it through Mexico,
which is really like hell for Central American migrants," Luiselli
told *Democracy Now!* (Goodman 2017). Central American vulnerability along the hazardous Mesoamerican route has been widely
explored in academic studies, journalistic feature and news writ-
ings, films, and documentaries (see Sandoval-García 2017; Basok
2015; Mártinez 2013; "Travelers in Hiding" 2012; *Sin Nombre*
2009; *Which Way Home* 2009; Nazario 2007). Anyone who cross-
es over has more than made it. Their perseverance across borders
is "life beyond life": "Survival is not simply that which remains but
the most intense life possible" (Derrida 2007, 52).

Problem Children

Communication scholars Timothy L. Sellnow and Matthew W.
Seeger outline that crises connote unpredictable, threatening, and
high-uncertainty occurrences bringing about a sense of collapse,
disruption, and harm (2003, 2, 4). These exigencies can include
the humanities crisis; an existential breakdown or midlife crisis;
a social crisis; a health crisis or pandemic; natural disasters like
earthquakes, tsunamis, tornadoes, and hurricanes; environmental
catastrophes like lead seeping into drinking water, global warming, drought, nuclear disaster, and an oil spill; financial disasters;
an energy crisis; terrorist attacks; or a "specific, unexpected, non-
routine event or series of events that create high levels of uncertainty and a significant or perceived threat to high priority goals"

(6–7). "The dizzying array of crisis narratives," as anthropologist Janet Roitman alludes to them, determines "the post hoc judgment of deviation, of failure" (2014, 41–42). The LatinX child migrant is a visually excessive sign of repetitive crisis and failure. The LatinX minor's forecast is gloomy: it is a futurity that cannot be. LatinX kids are a liability and tend to meet with the same kind of ending. Can one imagine what a Central American child in crisis can become? Can a LatinX child move beyond alienness? Perhaps 2014 indicates a bigger extremity: that of Central American negation, the disavowal of their humanness.

How did this grave U.S. emergency resonate in Central America? Public discourse of a state of crisis propelled Óscar Martínez to report on the phenomenon. The investigative journalist's account—"Los niños no se van: Se los llevan" ("The Children Don't Leave: They Take Them")—questions the perceived homogeneous entity of the "unaccompanied child migrant." His extraordinary article from July 2014 has not yet been published in English, and so I have translated all the excerpts referenced here. Martínez pushes for greater interpretive complexity vis-à-vis the decisions Central Americans make to move and engage in what still amounts to an open future. His piece tracks down the nuances within contexts of violence, family separation, and the business of human smuggling.

Martínez avoids the term crisis: it dehumanizes the Central American minor's perils and trauma. Children are not a crisis. "What has changed in the last few months," he asks, "so that tens of thousands of Central American children flee from violence?" Martínez infers that "if El Salvador's children would leave because of the violence alone, thousands and thousands would've left. We've been violent for a long time before fifty-two thousand children left." He consults with the pseudonymous "Señor Coyote," who has been in the human smuggling business since 1979. Mr. Coyote "boasts being one of El Salvador's first coyotes. When he began to *coyotear*," or smuggle, "he even ran ads for 'safe travel to the United States' on newspaper pages, listing his office number." Mr. Coyote's métier entails making headway through Mexico, getting the children to the other side, and training them "to forget they went with a coyote" (Martínez 2014).

More remarkable is a point made almost en passant, proffering insights about a LatinXness in transit and its temporary identifications. Mr. Coyote mentions that "many children passed through with the papers of Puerto Ricans or Dominicans." Martínez does not untangle the degrees of otherness that Central American children undertake at geographic and cultural crossroads and in an active process of "Latinization." Their modifications touch on a LatinXness of being: minors must "forget" about the adults guiding them from point X to point X and assume an accompanying "citizenship" from another country. Puerto Rican or Dominican papers facilitate the Central American child's mobility farther north, uprooting the child from his or her "origins," but beginning again as something else. These documents assign another layer of meaning to the LatinX minor (Martínez 2014).

Can we even quantify the dizzying array of Latin copiousness in these "Puerto Rican" and "Dominican" border crossings? What do we make of this deracinated but dispersed, "underage" but legal, and hidden but well-paced "Latinidad"—or, rather, these legal iterations of Dominicanness and Puerto Ricanness in Mesoamerica? Puerto Rican U.S. citizenships circulating through Mesoamerican undocumented migrations intimate broad "alien" movements. Puerto Ricans are U.S. citizens, of course, and the domain of a flexible Puerto Ricanness in this Central American moment punctuates a paradoxical "foreignness." An often-unrecognized U.S. citizenship is activated through the transitory "Americanness" of Central Americans. The LatinX migrant, hailing from elsewhere, is "naturalized" to other homelands. Martínez imparts another kind of resistance to restrictions that carve out family spaces. "If parents don't have a real choice to take their children in a legal way," he concludes, "if parents don't see that violence shows signs of declining significantly in Honduras, Guatemala, or El Salvador, if many of those parents no longer wash dishes but have established, after years of sacrifice, their own business, then what? If the United States, Guatemala, El Salvador, or Honduras does not give them an option, a coyote will give it to them. Parents will always want to have their children by their side" (Martínez 2014).

Central American movements continue. They are about far more than immigration forms. *Tell Me How It Ends* is, sure, about the comprehensive American questionnaire and its cultivation of alien personae. Luiselli tells us, in this sense, how the LatinX child begins: in movement, in deportation, in questions, and in new affiliations. The LatinX child is starting another production of meaning. The LatinX child is beginning here and there.

Numerosities

X'S INDEFINITE QUALITY impacts a major concern of our time: the unthought-of scale and impact of environmental degradation, paired with new forms of LatinX displacements and transitions. The intensity and uncertainty of global climate disruption are canvassed to comprehend ecological crises through extreme LatinX currents including border fortification, rising sea levels, Central America's drought, disintegrating bodies and landscapes, and Mesoamerican movements. The slow accretions and modifications of what comes into and goes out of existence—our own managing to eke out a living through "contaminated survival" (Casid 2018, 243)—encourages us to think expansively about unpredictable LatinX turning points.

My ideas on these themes come in the form of four sections. The first part begins with "Projections, Extremes, Transitions" and considers perilous scenarios for 2050: altered environments, urgent circumstances for the now, and an unrecognizable LatinXness. Next, I probe a "Transfixing X-ness": how the topsy-turvies of the present are throwing us headlong into LatinX's ubiquitous and unfolding patterns and the conceptual language trying to register the new nature of things. The penultimate section—"The X Corridor"—evokes literary scholar Steve Mentz's notion of climatologically "being in the brown," an uncontrollable brownness signaling what LatinX is becoming (2013). I wrap up with a rumination on the not-so-subrosa X as "The Time of Our Lives," advancing a reflective understanding of LatinX life in the twenty-first century.

Environmental literary studies, ecocriticism, and representations of nature, pastoral life, wilderness, or protected habitats greatly instruct but do not ground this approach (see Adamson and Slovic

2009; Nixon 2013; Acosta 2015; Solis Ybarra 2016; Wald, Solis Ybarra, Vázquez, and Ray 2019). I set my sights on postulating our LatinX moment and ecocide, as exemplified in other literary and vivid worlds of timely information: nonfiction, chronicles, news items, historical accounts, and online venues documenting the cataclysms of the bewildering and fickle now. These detailed layers—or, environments, if you wish—of human expression, interaction, and investigation are placed at the political forefront. They can be read as unrestrained preludes that help us move through and grasp a range of inchoate feelings, puzzlement, and contradictions.

These clusters of elaboration are told and retold to arrive at, if not rework, tangible orientations on LatinX life and its relationship to biophilia. Paul Lussier, Director of the Yale Science Communications with Impact Network, strategizes to make planetary care palatable to the U.S. public. He finds there is "an enormous opportunity to see and view and treat climate change as nothing but essentially a big, huge house of narratives that we can all connect to" (Halley 2018). LatinX narrative maneuvers meet the environment's gravity head on—keying into how it is being observed, experienced, and represented at this specific point of human history.

These stories' relevance dialogue with the world. They take great strides to understand contemporary transitions and vulnerability in a time when many people are living with shorter attention spans. The worth of attention becomes more valuable because it is turning out to be more and more scarce. These anecdotes bring out a speaker's idiosyncrasies, alongside the human nature of emotions, feelings, fear, and social connections. They can be captured through vernacular practices, what Mexican American writer Sandra Cisneros marshals through the expression, "me desahogué hablando contigo." Or, as she translates this saying, "I un-drowned talking to you" (Cisneros 2019). Storytelling forces us to listen very deeply and reach across communities. In Cisneros's words, "We're telling a story that's too powerful it comes out of our eyes" (Stasio 2019). They help us "to understand the event," to comprehend it for ourselves, and "to survive the event" (Stasio

2019). The transcription of X furthering this approach—from the digital to the real life—forges a LatinX subjectivity that circulates in a world as a deracinated LatinX. It is a purposeful house of X events and progressions, and "the spontaneous connections generated" through X users—X chroniclers—as conceptual artist R. Galvan might remind us, "lift it to new meaning[s]" (2017, 190).

This prolegomenon attempts to put the world together through LatinX uncertainty—a speculative mode that is thinking with the day-to-day and my willingness to follow the X's flow through the risky unknown. One is not literally Latin or X. Yet the X of today and its vagility are doubtlessly tied to a Latino/a future. I strive to make an opening for LatinX's fuller potential and scales, to be more than just a casual observer, and to construct systems of knowledge through what climate change and the X are doing.

Projections, Extremes, Transitions

Census projections demonstrate the United States is changing into a "Majority Minority Nation" (Taylor and Cohn 2012). By 2050, it is said, the United States will cease having "a clear white majority" (Goldstein 2016). The Latino/a population is expected to compose an estimated 106 million by the mid-twenty-first century—almost "double what it is today"—and grow into the largest U.S. majority-minority ethnoracial group (Krogstad 2014).

But there is another forecast looming for 2050, as border security and migration journalist Todd Miller spotlights in his eye-opening environmental investigation, *Storming the Wall: Climate Change, Migration, and Homeland Security* (2017). It is an alarming approximation on a global scale. The United Nations (U.N.) calculates that 250 million people will be displaced as a result of unraveling environmental processes such as rising sea levels, superstorms, damaging floods, flood-induced landslides, drought, desertification, drinking water shortages, agricultural disruption, and "multiple ecological factors projected to dislocate unprecedented quantities of people" (21–22).

Hold that thought: unheard-of quantities of climate refugees, or per the U.N., "persons of concern," from a bevy of geographies engaging in cross-border movement due to escalating environmental destabilization and turmoil (Miller 2017, 22). Not only this, but as Miller also contends, "there is more spending on border reinforcement than ever before in the history of humankind. And as the Donald J. Trump administration takes power in the United States, there is only more of this to come" (24). Anthropologist and theorist Nicholas De Genova underscores that border surveillance and militarization function in a "de facto process of artificial selection." Under the state's watchful eye, deadly obstacle routes "sort out the most able-bodied, disproportionately favoring the younger, stronger, and healthier among prospective (labor) migrants, and likewise inordinately favoring men over women" (25). "Unauthorized" migration, De Genova makes known, is recast "into a treacherous, death-defying endurance test, the autonomy and subjectivity of migration is subjected to what is merely the beginning of a long apprenticeship into a lifelong career of arduous exploitation" (25). Following Miller, we should not lose sight of the links among border enforcement, environmental stress, and population movements. In brief: "this is 'a situation of border fortification in a warming world,' a warming world where there is no legal protection for families who are suddenly displaced due to climate" (29).

These numerosities of people—a global ensemble and social expansion "proliferating across the world," to cite Miller's urgent point—"assault" the Global North with their "illegal" presence and with climate change as an abstract and suspect explanation (2017, 26). Do note this *Washington Post* headline, bringing this distrustful but pressing topic to the fore: "The U.S. Has More Climate Skeptics than Anywhere Else on Earth" (Erickson 2017). Repudiating environmental deterioration also means rejecting what the rest of the world is living. This national and climatological "browning" will reach its vertex in 2050 and displace not just the "clear white majority," but everything that has been conceived as "normal." The apogee of this browning signifies that the Earth is literally changing color. It is entering an era that biogeographer and ecologist Camilo Mora christens as a "climate departure," indicating that, by 2047, weather conditions "will become like something we've never seen" (Toomey 2014). But there is a kind of U.S. departure, too, as segments of the nation are becoming like something we have never seen, and the Earth metamorphoses into an other—beginning anew as something else.

The environmental outlet *Grist* published that a group of polar scientists have concluded that the Arctic "is now definitively trending toward an ice-free state" (Holthaus 2018). Peter Wadhams's scholarly undertaking *A Farewell to Ice* emphasizes that this zone's shifts are "not just an interesting change in a remote part of the world" (2017, 4). "We have created an ocean where there was once an ice sheet," he proclaims. "It is Man's first major achievement in reshaping the face of his planet, and it is of course an unintended achievement, with dubious and possibly catastrophic consequences to follow" (2–3). Wadhams's findings on the "Arctic death spiral" manifest "a spiritual impoverishment of the Earth," as "Arctic Ocean sea ice [. . .] once protected us from the impacts of climatic extremes" (4). "Let It Go," *Grist* announced, "the Arctic will never be frozen again" (Holthaus 2018). It "is our glimpse of an Earth in flux, transforming into something that's radically different from today." The online magazine averred that the polar region's permutations warrant a new term—the "New Arctic"—highlighting "the 'huge impact' these changes [are] having on everything from tourism to fisheries to worldwide weather patterns. 'What happens in the Arctic doesn't stay in the Arctic—it affects the rest of the planet'" (Holthaus 2018).

LatinX urbanity is facing this impact. Miami, the low-lying "U.S. Capital of Latin America," as the city is nicknamed, could be perishing as we know it by 2037, due to rising sea levels, a porous limestone foundation, and its topographical flatness (Goodell 2017). Limestone "is sedimentary rock formed from skeleton fragments of marine organisms like corals and mollusks. The ground under Miami is like a giant coral sponge" (Dawson 2017, 18). And "no one can turn a blind eye to the projections everyone uses in South Florida: 2 feet of sea-level rise by 2060" (Bolstad 2017).

It will not end there: sea levels are estimated to rise up to 6.6 feet by 2100, as predicted by the National Oceanic and Atmospheric Administration (Dawson 2017, 18). There is no place to hide in "Aguatica," as poet Victor Hernández Cruz would rather call Earth, where there is more water than terra firma (2017). The U.S. descendants of climate refugees—or, the next generation of LatinXs—confront what their families left behind. The X of human-caused disasters is never remote from the U.S. mainland: Latin lives, anecdotes, creations, and urban landscapes may be lost, submerged, environmentally crossed, or X'ed out in such a way that this "new" Miami could turn to a place of forgotten Latinness. Public records, land deeds, historical documents, and Latin special collections may be lost. Research by university archivists and climate scientists shows that material artifacts within the national archival infrastructure—manuscripts, codices, printed books, and so on—are at risk of degradation because of environmental disasters (Yeo 2018). What is the Latin familiar and cultural heritage in this context? The rising tides meet the city's cultural demands: even the environment requires Miami's attention.

Another LatinX scene with many stories may surface—a new beginning and remaking of LatinXness, LatinX social networks, and an altering world map that have yet to be known. Jesse M. Keenan, a researcher on urban development and climate adaptation at Harvard University's Graduate School of Design, proposed that "climate gentrification" has hit the Latin metropolis. Since 2000, "a correlation between elevation and price appreciation" illustrates an "early signaling of preference for properties at higher elevations and a reaction to persistent nuisance flooding in lower areas" (Schouten 2017). The effects of Miami's real estate market will spark migration from high-exposure areas and cause displacement, punctuating what can be conceived as the urban borders of climate change. Miami's Little Haiti—which lies on higher ground, approximately ten feet above sea level, and is less likely to flood—is a center of interest. Keenan states that, "In Miami, it's the reverse of the process in many other parts of the United States, or even in the developing world, where the poorest people to flooding and sea-level rise often live on low ground most vulnerable to flooding" (Bolstad 2017).

As climate gentrification establishes a firmer stronghold—and makes historically mixed-income areas more exclusive—Keenan upholds that it will be easy to "predict who the winners will be: wealthier people" (Schouten 2017). This struggle for livable space—what eco-criticism scholar Ashley Dawson dubs as an "exclusionary zone of refuge"—exhibits extremes in economic disparity, physical displacement, capacity for survival, and, for those in real estate, entrepreneurial opportunities (2017, 8). As global sociologist Saskia Sassen frames it, "For those at the bottom or in the poor middle, this means expulsion from a life space; among those at the top, this appears to have meant exiting from the responsibilities of membership in society via self-removal, extreme concentration of the wealth available in a society, and no inclination to redistribute that wealth" (2014, 15). It is not so much ethnicity that is marketable in the spatial politics of this "new" Miami, but a private property's elevation. It cedes, at the ground level, a particular hue: an urban dark "brown for the poor," to riff off design writer Kassia St. Clair's reveries in *The Secret Lives of Color* (2016, 239).

This brown for the poor touches on what little remains, and perilously so, throughout the world and who is accessing those resources. Cape Town, to date, is dangerously close to "Day Zero." South Africa's second-most populous urban area is projected to run out of water, becoming "one of the few major cities in the world to lose piped water to homes and most businesses" (Onishi and Sengupta 2018). Its four million residents "may have to stand in line surrounded by armed guards to collect rations of the region's most precious commodity: drinking water" (Welch 2018). Stricter allocations amidst extinction-level water crises, the *New York Times* informed, "is a difficult message to convey in one of the world's most unequal societies, where access to water reflects

Cape Town's deep divisions. In squatter camps, people share com-
munal taps and carry water in buckets to their shacks. In other
parts of the city, millionaires live in mansions with glistening
pools" (Onishi and Sengupta 2018). On a global scale, more than
"one billion people lack access to water and another 2.7 billion find
it scarce for at least one month of the year." The BBC explained
that Cape Town is just the tip of the iceberg. Other major cities
facing water stress include São Paulo, Brazil; Bangalore, India;
Beijing, China; Cairo, Egypt; Jakarta, Indonesia; Moscow, Russia;
Istanbul, Turkey; Mexico City, Mexico; London, England; Tokyo,
Japan; and Miami, Florida (BBC 2018).

In the historically agricultural region of the Mexicali Valley,
farmers are confronting a drought and contesting the one billion
dollar production plans and infrastructure project of a major U.S.
brewery, Constellation Brands, producer of Modelo and Corona
beers (Dibble 2018). The company is threatening Mexicali's water resources, setting out to consume "20 million liters of drinking
water every year: the same amount that would normally quench
the thirst of some 750,000 people" (teleSur 2018). Since 2010
Mexico "overtook the Netherlands to become the world's biggest
beer exporter," and "breweries have sprung up across its arid borderlands" (Agren 2018). The Mexicali manufacturer is scheduled
for a 2020 opening—initially yielding "58 million cases of beer
each year and go[ing] on to produce quadruple that amount in the
future" (Dibble 2018). "The twenty-first century has an analogue,"
world historian Raj Patel and sociologist Jason W. Moore remind
us. "It's easier for most people to imagine the end of the planet
than to imagine the end of capitalism" (2017, 2).

This could all be giving way by 2050—or, even way before it—to
the unavoidable, as Finnish author Emmi Itäranta's fable conjectures it, to the *Memory of Water* (2014). This terrifying prognosis
can also startle and interrupt cultural events that otherwise help
us escape a frenzied daily life and bring us relative pleasure and
harmony. Such was the case when I was at a concert by Brazilian
American singer Bebel Gilberto, who paused in the middle of a

number to pose a question that cannot be downplayed: "You know we're going to be without water?" (Gilberto 2018). There is no safe moment now, Gilberto intimated, as her music became a part of the background, and as we waited—in our togetherness, in the grand stage of human history and emotions—for what will be thrown our way. We will not survive unscathed.

A 2016 report by the Natural Resources Defense Council (NRDC), a non-profit environmental policy group, noted that Latinos, Latinas, LatinXs are "vulnerable to climate-related threats," depending on their U.S. geographies. The account specified that "more than 60 percent of U.S. Latinos live in California, Texas, Florida, and New York, which are among the states most vulnerable to severe heat, air pollution, and flooding." "Nationally," NRDC elaborated, "Hispanics are 21 percent more likely than non-Hispanic whites to live in the hottest parts of cities, which have a high concentration of heat-retaining surfaces and little to no tree cover. More than 24 million Hispanics live in the 15 U.S. cities most heavily polluted by ozone smog, including Los Angeles, Houston, and New York. In Florida, Hispanics make up about 40 percent of the population in the eight Florida cities (including Miami) that will almost certainly flood during future high tides, no matter how quickly the world cuts the carbon pollution driving sea level rise" (Quintero and Constible 2016, 5).

This climatological browning gives rise to a tension in a twofold way. On the one hand, it is an additive, as in coming into a space and the expanding nature of the LatinX population. And, on the other, this browning is subtractive: meaning, the diminishing fertility and fecundity through climatological change generating, as biologist and conservationist Rachel Carson observed, "browned and withered vegetation as though swept by fire" ([1962] 2002, 3). A brownness of devastation—brown water, musty-smelling brown sludge, brown mountains, brown piles of debris, and brownouts—as seen in Puerto Rico during the September 2017 torrential downpours of Hurricane Maria, a Category 4 storm with 155 mph winds. Hurricane Maria's ravage brought about "the largest

scale psychosocial disaster in the United States" (Fichter 2017).
Living through and surviving these types of superstorms create
anxiety and trauma: "diagnosable mental disorders" that are common "among combat veterans and those who live through mass
shootings and natural disasters" (Calma 2017; see Holpuch 2018).
Human recovery goes hand-in-hand with the ongoing restoration
of Puerto Rico's infrastructure (Fichter 2017). While the location
and strength of hurricanes may vary, the words of a Rockaway,
Queens, resident who was affected by Hurricane Sandy in 2012
carry weight: "If you dodge one season, you just don't know what
will happen next time" (Calma 2017).

You just don't know what will happen next time . . . or how, exactly, you will be hit. In another extraordinary turn of life events, this
same storm brought an incredulous transformation for Marvin
Rosales Martinez, a Salvadoran landscaper. He was raking "leaves
on a Long Island street after Hurricane Sandy" when he hit the
jackpot by coming across "a million-dollar winning lottery tick-
et" (Valentine and Mongelli 2013). The New York State Gaming
Commission honored his "Win $1,000 a Week for Life" scratch
card. It is ironic that good fortune is masked in the detritus of this
deluge, one that is only uncovered by the Salvadoran's labor. There
is astonishment, too, at seeing a Salvadoran presence of fortune
rather than misfortune—a warming up, for a brief moment, to a
U.S. Central American body. But if the Salvadoran perpetuates the
continuous myth of winning, it's worth recollecting that the lottery houses more losers.

Even so, an arbitrariness emerges through trash, paper scraps,
and the New York sweepstakes. The scrappy migrant is no longer
figurative rubbish, as the waste he encounters in his routine work
produces a miracle story. The LatinX hand with the LatinX eye exca-
vates this LatinX moment. But the landscaper must first go through
the trash to change his luck. He receives attention not for his skills,
but because his riches, amidst chaos, have turned him into a valuable
American. Life has suddenly been made easier. This gathering-zone
presents a different "origin" for the Salvadoran migrant, or a new

AmericanX remade by—and in—disaster. His AmericanXness and LatinXness have an atypical beginning. A new AmericanX myth and a new LatinX figure are inaugurated through two unwanted U.S. subject matters: climate change and the omnipresent Latino/a migrant. Climatological *and* American excess produce this odd yet fantastic LatinX occurrence: literal junk and the otherwise "illegal" migrant mute into scattered, unmanageable stuff.

Miller writes that "just as every climate projection show[s] more environmental crisis, market projections for homeland security reveal a world where Big Brother will continue to dominate" (2017, 109). With shrinking resources—and in a twenty-first century planet of "Category 6 winds, ravaging fires, devouring seas, and parched landscapes"—environmental crises, surveillance, and barricaded parts of the world "are poised to become a part of people's everyday lives in ways that they have never been before" (Miller, 109). The Category 6 designation is used "as an unofficial category given to a hurricane so powerful that it breaks the scale": it is a label that attempts to grasp "the vast planetary changes" from 2017 alone (Yoder 2017). Border enforcement is the evidence of a browning that is out of hand. The Mesoamerican corridor is on the radar as "a major area of homeland security risk," because "more frequent severe droughts and tropical storms, especially in Mexico, Central America, and the Caribbean could increase population movements, both legal and illegal, toward or across the U.S. border" (69).

At the turn of the twenty-first century, Uruguayan author Eduardo Galeano penned an op-ed titled, "An SOS from the South," where he avowed, "Central America will soon count its trees like a bald man counts the hairs on his head" (2002). Central America's Northern Triangle is not generally viewed as the bearer of good tidings and has been facing a severe drought. Known as the Dry Corridor—or, in Spanish, *Corredor Seco*—this area is mainly on the Pacific littoral and extends from Chiapas, Mexico, to Panama. Guatemala, Honduras, and El Salvador are recognized as a central part of this Dry Corridor, housing about 10.5 million people. As Miller resonantly puts it, the Dry Corridor is "ground zero for global warming's impact in the

Americas" (2017, 75). Environmental writers John R. Wennersten and Denise Robbins clarify that "the Dry Corridor is cut off from ocean humidity by mountain ranges in the Caribbean, which create a rain shadow. The region experiences dry seasons that last longer than those in surrounding areas and is vulnerable to drought when its already short rainy season is reduced by El Niño—or by climate change" (2017, 107).

El Faro recounted that the drought made it impossible to grow corn, beans, and rice: the main staples of a Central American diet. Take note of these 2015 figures shared by the renowned Salvadoran digital publication: "In Guatemala, some 300,000 families are affected, in El Salvador more than 100,000 producers, in Nicaragua there's a water shortage and basic crops have been lost, as in Costa Rica, where hundreds of cattle died in the country's north and $250 million dollars were lost in agricultural exports." "We are facing an unprecedented calamity," is how the Honduran mayor of Texiguat characterized his environment (Leiva 2015). Texiguat is a municipality on the Dry Corridor with 12,000 residents, of which 80 percent live in extreme poverty.

Per the U.N.'s Food and Agriculture Organization (FAO), the region has undergone "one of the worst droughts of the last ten years with over 3.5 million in need of humanitarian assistance," a meteorological pattern that will affect food and nutrition security ("Drought in the Dry Corridor of Central America" n.d.). More than that, the Dry Corridor's area may be expanding. In Honduras, it "has nearly tripled in size over the past three decades," covering almost 45 percent of national territory, whereas previously the *Corredor Seco* was "limited to the extreme south of the country, near the Nicaraguan border" (Wennersten and Robbins 2017, 110). Writer Lauren Markham disseminated Central American figures from Climatelinks, a project of the United States Agency for International Development, in a *New York Times* op-ed. "The average temperature in El Salvador has risen 2.34 degrees Fahrenheit since the 1950s," she revealed, "and droughts have become longer and more intense. The sea has risen by three inches since the

1950s, and is projected to rise seven more by 2050. Between 2000 and 2009, 39 hurricanes hit El Salvador, compared with 15 in the 1980s. This, too, is predicted to get worse" (2018).

Journalistic boilerplates of the migrant caravan exodus focused on Northern Triangle individuals who were fleeing, as Associated Press journalist Sonia Perez D. referenced it, "widespread poverty, lack of opportunity, and rampant gang violence as their motivation" (2019). The *Guardian* zeroed in on another underlying layer—"The Unseen Driver behind the Migrant Caravan: Climate Change"—forcing farmers off their land in countries like Honduras, the world's third largest coffee producer. Unpredictable weather patterns and the climate change-related roya fungus—or, coffee rust disease—have impelled farmers to "first migrate to urban areas, where they confront a new set of problems, which in turn prompt them to consider an international odyssey" (Milman, Holden, and Agren 2018; Visram 2018).

"A warming climate has allowed the coffee rust to spread to plants in higher elevations" in Honduras, the *Washington Post* made known, "and farmers have to invest in medicines to keep their plants healthy" (Leutert 2018). It usually takes up to three years for coffee trees to mature, and, for coffee workers, this means not being able to earn income for three years (Visram 2018). Writer John Washington and photographer Tracie Williams delineated that besides Northern Triangle migrants, Mexicans, Nicaraguans, Venezuelans, Somalis, Cameroonians, and Brazilians, among others, were joining the U.S.-bound exodus and seeking asylum (Washington and Williams 2018). Given the projected numerosities of climate refugees by 2050, "a new international framework will be needed to accommodate them"—one that centers on "the needs of displaced people, rather than their exact reason for leaving" (Milman, Holden, and Agren 2018).

Farmers—*campesinos*, or "earth workers," who "survive exclusively on the fruits of the earth" (Andréu 2014)—are among the thousands of families "who have to do miracles to eat, to stretch a few eggs, beans, and tortillas" (Peña 2016). Recall here, too, Maya groups like Guatemala's Mam population, whose elders teach their families and communities how to till their land based on a precise knowledge of the weather. This traditional know-how is becoming more and more of a challenge, as "the climate is dramatically changing," and small family farms—or, *milpas*—are turning out to be unproductive (Fernandes 2018). There are no markets in some of these indigenous towns. These families' daily meals come directly from the *milpa*, and since "the subsistence farming isn't providing enough to feed" them, "chronic malnutrition is a grave risk for small children" (Fernandes 2018). A primary school teacher in a Guatemalan village stressed that "learning is a real challenge because many of his littlest students are malnourished" (Fernandes). A Harvard University study cautioned that as climate change worsens, the world's food supply will be less nutritious due to rising carbon-dioxide levels (Medek, Schwartz, and Myers 2017). By 2050, the scientific research concluded, 1.4 billion people will be in peril of protein deficiency, an estimate that includes "613.6 million people at risk in sub-Saharan Africa, 276.4 million in India, 131.7 million in Eastern and Southeast Asia and the Pacific, 84.4 million in Central Latin America and the Caribbean, and 77.8 million elsewhere in South Asia" (Medek, Schwartz, and Myers).

As Galeano imparted, "The greater the amount of farmland in the world that goes to rack and ruin, the more fertilisers and pesticides have to be used" (Galeano 2002). News stories from a few years back encapsulate these emergencies exacerbated by the lack of rain. A 2014 lead in Reuters bore the headline, "Drought Leaves up to 2.81 Mln Hungry in Central America—U.N." (Palencia), while a 2016 article pronounced, "El Salvador Declares Drought Emergency for First Time Ever" (Reuters Staff). This drying—pegged as a "silent crisis" (del Rincón 2015)—"could descend into drought-fueled conflicts at any moment" in parts of Central America and Mexico, as a Columbia University ocean and climate physicist put it (Bawden 2015). FAO calculations from 2016 found that 1.6 million people faced food insecurity in the Dry Corridor and that 3.5 million individuals needed humanitarian assistance (FAO 2016). The dry weather—"leav[ing] humanity home-less" (Galeano 2002)—is regarded as the main reason Central Americans are fleeing the isthmus: "because of hunger and a lack of food than over fears of crime and gang violence," as the *Miami Herald* summed it up (Welsh 2017). But there is not just literal hunger. Non-figurative thirst arises, too. Drought and hunger-driven migration become "'the ultimate coping strategy' [. . .] an option people turn to when they have no other choice" (Welsh).

Central American mobilities can be grasped through a new log-ic of expulsion, as Sassen deems it (2014). These expulsions can "range from elementary policies to complex institutions, systems, and techniques that require specialized knowledge and intricate or-ganizational formats" (2014, 2). Sassen elucidates, "What marks the specificity of our current period is that we have extracted so many resources from our planet and pushed so many people and whole communities off their land to do so, that this extractive logic is now becoming highly visible. This extractive mode has also generated new types of migrations. And it is not clear to me how this all ends, but it can't be very good" (Sassen and Torino 2017). The inequalities exacerbated by extractive modes might signify that the acceleration of environmental destruction can have serious implications for those in the Northern Triangle engaged in indigenous land rights.

Honduras, to an exceptional degree, holds the "inglorious ranking" as the deadliest nation in the world "for environmen-tal and land activists, particularly those from indigenous groups" (Lakhani 2016; Watts 2015). Berta Cáceres—a Honduran indige-nous and environmental rights campaigner and recipient of the 2015 Goldman Environmental Prize, the world's leading award honoring grassroots environmentalists—was murdered in 2016 for her "high-profile campaigns against dams, illegal loggers, and plantation owners" (Watts 2016). After receiving the Goldman Prize, Cáceres stated in an interview that environmental activists are at great "risk because they are up against powerful political and economic interests who have grown used to exploiting their land with impunity" (Watts 2015).

She added: "These are centuries-old ills, a product of domina-
tion. There is a racist system in place that sustains and reproduces
itself. The political, economic, and social situation in Honduras is
getting worse and there is an imposition of a project of domina-
tion, of violent oppression, of militarisation, of violation of human
rights, of transnationalisation, of the turning over of the riches and
sovereignty of the land to corporate capital, for it to privatise energy, the rivers, the land; for mining exploitation; for the creation of
development zones" (Watts 2015). Cáceres's body stands contrary
to the Honduran "natural" order established by the government
and corporate goals. Her body, it can be said, is in the way. It is
not sufficient to merely expel it from the land. It must be deprived
of life itself, much like the land, or, in few words, dead bodies for
the Northern Triangle's "dead land." To consult Sassen: a surge of
foreign land acquisitions means that "more land and water need to
be acquired to replace what has died" (2014, 149).

Transfixing X-ness

With 2050 close at hand, we are approaching a point—as these
forecasts and violence of the present moment attest to—where
displacement will continue to become a normal. There is an increasing LatinX population and a decreasing place for it to be. To
summon philosopher Thomas Nail's assertion, "with respect to
movement, displacement is not a lack but a positive capacity or
trajectory (even if the empirical outcome is not desirable)" (2015,
12). Globality and deracination attend to this other kind of mobility—a cognitive rebooting of sorts that amounts to a "translation"
under Nail's analytic gaze. It is an immediate making sense of the
world as people attempt to cast their former understanding of
themselves into the current moment more deeply.

The swift emergence of the untidy designation evinces that
LatinX is happening—thriving—at this time. Its breakthrough has
displaced the U.S. Latina and Latino labels. The otherworldliness
of the here and now suggests that Latina and Latino continuity

cannot be easily attached to LatinX's magnitude. Think of it as a constellation of entirely different X ideas making spaces for uncertainties and tensions that are not reducible to ontological bodies. LatinX, as a symbolic nexus, questions conventional groupings of Latin, Latino/a, Latina/o, and Latin@.

To engage with the field of Latin*X* Studies is to observe and tackle a series of unfolding transitions precisely through that X: a shape-shifting X. This X is not so much what Latino/Latina/Latin "is," but what and where it is moving toward, what it may become, and what it could inhabit. X as a transition—as a different genealogy—for this "Transition Era."

This is a contemporary transition period that, environmentally speaking, dovetails with our X-ness of the now and that has not been properly or vividly captured by extant vocabulary—at least according to the President of Oxford Dictionaries. He explained that during the 2017 "Word of the Year" season, there was a scarcity of terms regarding environmental changes. "News cycles brimmed with coverage of permafrost and glaciers melting, the never-ending debate over climate change, and the devastating effects of hurricanes that battered islands and coasts alike," he expressed. As their Word of the Year "process got underway we scoured the language corpora for a 2017 coinage giving voice to Mother Nature's anguish and wrath. Alas. We may have talked until we were arctic blue in the face, but we found no evidence of a new or re-emerging word that embodies what's happening to the Earth. Consider this a call to arms to all you self-styled neologists out there: coin that new word for 'Mother Nature's wrath.' We need it!" (Grathwohl 2017). Do we have a crisis in meaning? Are we lexically unprepared and lack the inventiveness to brainstorm, sculpt, or synthesize into a unified entity this catastrophic moment (or, to formulate and culturally represent it in a way that merits the Oxford Dictionaries' attention and recognition)? But even if this word is devised—and we engage with that exigent term—we may be bringing forward problems that we may be unwilling and psychically unready to grapple with.

Uncertainty about the business of living may dictate one's trepidation in trying to create a new category for the global inescapableness of "Mother Nature's wrath." Sociologist Kari Marie Norgaard has tracked down how Norwegians who are knowledgeable of global warming distance themselves from its disastrous impact to evade the unsettling reactions emanating from this dark matter. Some in this Scandinavian country construct "boundaries of thought" and a "sense of normal everyday life" (2011, 5–6). The Norwegians interviewed—in Norgaard's efforts to forge a nexus among thinking, feeling, and the process of emotion management vis-à-vis environmental information—"described fears about the severity of climate change, of not knowing what to do, that their way of life was in question, and that the government would not adequately handle the problem. They described feelings of guilt for their own actions and the difficulty of discussing the issue of climate change with their children" (9).

A "production of denial regarding global warming" turns up in Norway, whose population is "among the most educated and environmentally minded people in the world" and "especially attuned to their natural environment" (Norgaard 2011, 10, 14, 21). Norgaard noticed that reactions to global warming brought about "tensions between vulnerability and security in daily life." This Norwegian community shed light on "a particularly pronounced tension between the known, ordered, safe universe of the town and the larger world around it. There was a desire to keep change out, including climate change, but nonlocal problems were sometimes hard to ignore" (21). That vibrant word pursued by the President of Oxford Dictionaries—whose perfected vocabulary will direct us to a new etymological narrative—may materialize anywhere. But perhaps the point in question is not that a word for "Mother Nature's anguish and wrath" is out of the realm of one's imagination. The vital concern may be that what is coming, in earth-shaking extremes, is not clear. It may remain unfathomable to our current language, and we may not necessarily want to find out (see Beeler 2018).

Still, this era of formation through climatological anguish and wrath already exists. The global-scale and enduring transformations to the Earth's prevailing state of affairs are being framed through the moniker Anthropocene—from the ancient Greek words *anthropos*, for "human being," and *kainos*, for "recent, new"—which replaces the Holocene. Paul Crutzen, a Nobel Prize-winning chemist, and biologist Eugene F. Stoermer proposed this term in 2000. The Anthropocene signifies that the present geological era of degradation is one triggered by humans. The environmental outcomes on the Earth system are marked by human imprints on the planet, affecting "the world's climate and biodiversity . . . its very geological structure, and not just for centuries, but for millennia" (Scranton 2015, 18). These key turning points are commonly grasped from the advent of the Industrial Revolution onward. The Anthropocene's precise start date is much contested, and alternative references have been proposed. For Jason W. Moore, colossal ecological crises need to be tied to the violence and inequality produced by capitalism, what he dubs "Capitalocene" (2015). Yet as a "geopolitical event," the Anthropocene is a resourceful concept for environmental shifts as it attempts to capture the role of humans in the natural world—excavating, as historians Christophe Bonneuil and Jean-Baptiste Fressoz assert, "how we got to this point" and "what is to be done" (2015, 24, 49).

The Anthropocene has antecedents. Theories of ecology, evolution, and biogeography have circulated as far back as the nineteenth century, or earlier—and with LatinX America as a stimulating naturalistic site (see Jackson 2009). German scientist, explorer, naturalist, and polymath Alexander von Humboldt's (1769–1859) insightful acuity conceptualized ecological relationships where climate was deemed an interconnected tapestry of landmass, altitude, weather, and oceans (Toomey 2016). Von Humboldt's expedition from 1799–1804 throughout Spanish colonial territories (today's Venezuela, Colombia, Ecuador, Peru, Mexico, and Cuba)—"penetrating deep into lands where few Europeans had ever gone before"—molded his idea of the web of life, or more generally, a vision of nature as we know it (Wulf 2016, 7). "When nature is perceived as a web," science-writing biographer Andrea Wulf proffers, "its vulnerability also becomes obvious. Everything hangs together. If one thread is pulled, the whole tapestry may unravel" (6).

Von Humbolt created a metaphoric unity between natural architecture—the web—and the environment writ large. Conceptual artist Mark Dion, recognized for his use of scientific presentations in his installations, maintains that von Humboldt instigates the notion "of the importance of moving through the landscape as a way of knowing" (Bilger and Rangel 2014, 101). His unified view of nature was bound by local and global scales—or, "global vegetation and climate zones"—laying down defining components that "helped create modern environmentalism" (Toomey 2016). Von Humbolt's approach, for Dion, makes him "'Scientist as everything': scientist as storyteller, scientist as adventurer, scientist as cosmologist, scientist as celebrity, scientist as educator, etc." (Bilger and Rangel 2014, 94). Present-day "ecologists, environmentalists, and nature writers rely" on his outlook, "although most do so unknowingly," as Wulf notes (2016, 9). Von Humboldt's charting of biological terra incognita is based on the "understudied" *LatinX* (see Rebok 2014). Unwittingly, this is a LatinX "beginning" through foreign material, distant landscapes, and life forms. LatinX is working through an understanding of nature as nature—or, rather, through our spiraling catastrophic relationship to nature, a simple survival instinct.

Climatological changes and LatinX spaces propel us to find a vocabulary for the unprecedented events of our time. Transitional processes, different in magnitude, are marked by changes that, as 2050 signals, range from minority to majority, from green earth to brown earth, from one space to another, from a complete body to a vanishing one, from Latino/a to LatinX. Transitions can occur suddenly and with little preparation: the Xs of exits, entries, and reentries. Transitional Xs are passing by and passing through Latin constellations. Transitions convey textual and cognitive movement. They proceed from one meaning to another, tracing ongoing thoughts in transition, adrift, perhaps, but on their way to becoming substantive expressions of thought.

This salient X could very well be the most powerful conceptual point of our moment, a matrix offering a way to tinker with the unfathomable and the unfamiliar. While on the subject of the "familiar," how does ontological brownness for U.S. Latinas and Latinos transition at this moment in time? Is ecological devastation releasing us from a brownness that is primarily summoned as representative of the Latin body? Climatic change is a more sophisticated understanding for the transitions that are happening to the environment—turning things, nations, and thronging masses into something unintelligible, or something else.

Whereas once we may have been thinking merely of migrations and increasing populations, we now have complete dislocations of "Latinness" and "Latin" individuals: an unrecognizable LatinXness. What does LatinX look like through climate change? We can no longer point to Latin America as the source and supplier of Latinness—or, to the United States as another provenance of Latinness—if Latinness, as we know, localize, and ground it, may no longer exist.

Environmental uncertainty presents a situation where deracination is taking over in a powerful and bone-chilling way. The "-ness" suffix in LatinX—shaping and advancing an abstract noun that denotes a quality and state of being—gets it just about right. The unsettledness behind LatinXness points us to whether or not we have an appetite—or, desire—to investigate what we ascribe meaning to. LatinX is not about how squarely, how "rightly," and how convincingly one fits into the Latino/a ontological category, but it is instead a marker of how one navigates the world.

LatinX's profundity and unknowableness is our shared contemporary situation. The gender-neutral denomination germinates from online communities, an internet connectivity that circulates in everyday life and that simultaneously necessitates a physical space in the "real" world as well as the scholarly field of Latino/a

Studies. I want to seize the implied obscure semiotics of the embraced "X" at the end of "Latin" and deliver it to other assemblages: the X of the unknown quantity of dark brown people hailing from the "Latin" world that is Central America's Northern Corridor. It is an X trying to come to terms with this new Central American age. This slippery and restless X is, and is not, ontological. The Northern Corridor's X-ness codes these X-bodies, one where the denial and rejection of global warming, the condemnation of the immigrant, and the abjection and socioeconomic inequality of the Central American all converge. Surveillance must be magnified for these omnifarious Xs—a vigilance indexed by Miller as "militarized borders, armed guards, [. . .] incarceration, and forced expulsions" (2017, 90).

These Central American migrants are, in a manner of speaking, discursively disfigured bodies in dangerous opposition to the U.S. citizenry's public welfare. A climatological disfigurement affects, if not alters, laboring bodies under extreme heat in humid areas. Approximately 20,000 inhabitants, whose métier lies in farming, sugarcane fields, fishing, or construction, in El Salvador's Bajo Lempa region, for instance, have been diagnosed with a new form of chronic kidney disease spreading through Central America and southern Mexico (Palmer 2017; see PBS NewsHour 2018). An article from the *Journal of Epidemiology and Community Health* expounded that El Salvador "has the highest overall mortality from kidney disease in the world (with Nicaragua and Honduras also included in the 10 highest countries)" (Ramirez-Rubio et al. 2013, 1). The cause of this kidney failure is undetermined, science journalist Jane Palmer highlights, but it is noteworthy that "the areas that have the highest solar radiation and heatwaves" coincide with "the places right where the epidemics are" (Palmer 2017).

The "unusual phenomenon," as National Public Radio described it, is also occurring in India and Sri Lanka. Cecilia Sorensen, who teaches at the University of Colorado School of Medicine, said that "It's very difficult to prove direct attribution and say this person is sick because of climate change. But what we can say is that this disease is occurring in parts of the world that are experiencing unprecedented warming, which we can attribute to climate change." Sorensen notes while there may be "multi-factorial" causes, "this form of kidney failure is only happening in places that are hot and muggy—and getting hotter" (Beaubien 2019).

Heat stress and dehydration damage the kidneys. Climate experts at the National Oceanic and Atmospheric Administration in Boulder, Colorado, find that this "may well be one of the first epidemics because of global warming." They "predict the kidney is going to be one of the prime targets as heat increases" (Palmer 2017). As Carson advanced in *Silent Spring*, "human health [. . .] ultimately reflect[s] the environment's ills" (Lear 2002, xvi). The Dry Corridor's agricultural workers are not just ailing bodies: they are "melting."

These LatinX fragments have ostensibly adapted to this environmental temporality—a not so subtle hint of their present and future displacement. "This is really a silent massacre," is how a Salvadoran kidney specialist described it (Palmer 2017). Central American bodies expose that to be in the Earth—and in this time— one is not a complete person, even as one tries to pick up the pieces of one's life. They force us to think about the sacrifice that may go into this kind of translation and mobility of the everyday—its starting point, sequence of journeys, and no definitive return—a course that tries to recover from the devastation but may be at the point of no return.

The X Corridor

Central America's "silent crisis" and "silent massacre" bring into being what we might understand as an X Corridor. Central American invisibility conjoins with the illusive climatological browning of the Earth that reinforces silence and an isolation of events. Perhaps more daunting is the possibility of a nearing silence activated by a contingent desertion of "all living things," to purloin from Carson's magnum opus ([1962] 2002, 3). This X springs forth from disintegrating landscapes, human lives and bodies, and everyday existence: the poignant X of the Dry Corridor's barrenness and desolation.

"The contemporary," philosopher Giorgio Agamben posits, is one who perceives the darkness of one's own time—a darkness that "never ceases to engage" (2009, 45). But this almost imperceptible X of "thick darkness" defies stagnancy, as the X being solicited is never fixed and may be "perpetually voyaging toward us" (46–47). "Our time, the present, is in fact not only the most distant: it cannot in any way reach us," Agamben emphasizes. "Its backbone is broken and we find ourselves in the exact point of this fracture. This is why we are, despite everything, contemporaries" (47). The X's unrest, all in all, "pulses . . . in the present" (50). Central America's disruption demands a line of sight, an analytic capacity to see dark things that are far from linear and neat. The interference that X problems generate are getting larger and larger. The X has sundry intersections, cycles, and lives of its own.

LatinXs in Mesoamerica's Dry Corridor are tackling new life forms. That X veers here to the Earth's browning problem, which exceeds national borders. Consider the pseudonymously christened Flores twins, unaccompanied minors who flee their fictionally named Salvadoran hometown of La Colonia because of gang violence and death threats, as portrayed in Lauren Markham's *The Far Away Brothers* (2017). Markham amends the siblings' names and Salvadoran neighborhood to protect their family from violent gang-related retribution. The identical brothers—"with their duplicate faces of fear," with "the same problem and the same face" (115, 119)—narrowly escape, the narrative suggests, drought and food insecurity. Yet their new geography's landscape—Oakland, California—paradoxically connects them to their farming family in Central America. Aboard public transportation one day, a sibling scrutinizes how the Oakland hillsides are "balding from thirst—the same drought, he knew, that was afflicting his family back in El Salvador" (221).

The twins' father informs them that "sometimes there was no

rain; sometimes the rain came at the wrong time," and he goes out, now and then, "to the land to pray" (Markham 2017, 249). Mr. Flores reports that his summer tomato crop from 2016 "was bad, due to a problem he'd never seen before." The tomatoes were "pallid in color, their skin a mottled orange-yellow" and "seen from far away, they were easily mistaken for citrus. He couldn't figure out what had gone wrong" (249). The brownness of the earth had dulled the vegetable's vibrancy, making it foreign to the Flores patriarch's eyes. The thing once so common and within his control is now peculiar. From far away, the husbandman may recognize the tomato, but only as something else, just as from far away—farthest away, even—the brothers and their father are now more comparable to being LatinX.

Mr. Flores cannot fathom what his efforts have yielded. The problem is so big he cannot recognize it, despite the fact that he's in the middle of it, and the evidence of the tomatoes' edges is in front of him. It is the farmer who is wrong, not the earth, when it is humans who have now made the earth "wrong." More daunting still is what may be happening to the Flores tract of land—or "dead land," as Sassen propositions. "Once land cannot be used anymore to extract natural resources," she bids, "it becomes invisible, even though it has a very visible material condition" (Sassen and Torino 2017). Ironically, the family's last name, Flores, meaning flowers, appears as a surviving memorial of something past: a plant life that once blossomed.

The twins may have fled their nation's gang violence, but the seemingly identical uncertainties in the climatological fluctuation of this brown stretch—of what comes with the brown earth—follows them to the North. As the Flores brothers attempt to navigate California, they endeavor to maneuver the Golden State's brownness, one that is not too remote from El Salvador. This browning, at this juncture, is one's home. A home of the unknown.

Literary scholar Steve Mentz writes that "we need brown but do not like looking at it. It is a color you cannot cover up, that will not go away." He goes on to say, "A color you cannot see through, brown captures a connecting opacity at the heart of ecological thinking. It comes at us from both sides of our world, the living and the dead. Brown marks the fertile soil that plants consume and the fecal waste that animals reject" (2013, 193). The dark brownness coming at us signals an enmeshed Central American corporeality and environment that are not separated. They are paradoxically yoked through an ecological "living potential and dead excess" (207). "To be ecological is to be brown, disturbingly," details Mentz (193). This brownness is not about being brown in a Latino or Latina sense as much as "being in the brown" (200). Being *in* this kind of brown means existing inescapably and almost uniformly in an assertive state of claiming the human and the world, when both seem beyond its bounds, and when one is invariably caught off guard by the increasing environmental crises at hand. Being within the brown is an out-of-control brownness, an earthly hue that is not so abstractly intimating what LatinX is becoming. When brownness will point, in 2050, to the desolation of the Earth, how does one handle brownness?

Being in the brown is—and is not—out of reach, as California's 2017 massive fires exhibited, turning some of the Golden State's neighborhoods into "piles of soot and concrete" (Chavez 2017). "What was once a paradise was like a war zone," Jeannette Frescas, a Ventura, California, resident, told CNN. "At midnight, I woke up with a flashlight in my face," she relayed. "I looked out my window and there were flames that were like, a hundred feet, all around us" (Chavez). In Sonoma and Napa counties, many LatinX undocumented workers that "tend vines, ferment wine, build homes, and feed tourists" were "among the worst hit by the fires that scorched over 190,000 acres and destroyed more than a dozen wineries." Reuters confirmed that there was "a huge flood of Latino evacuees to the coast" (Randewich and Henderson 2017).

Undocumented LatinXness must, once again, take flight. A Sonoma County resident commented that Latina and Latino "folks just went right past those shelters and they tried to get, I think, as far away from the fire as possible, but also beyond institutional help, on purpose." LatinX lives—being exigently *in* the brown—are beyond institutional recognition and assistance, for, in the end, what is the progression and the promise of a shared LatinX planetary life? The magnitude of LatinX activity is marked by inexhaustible capacity to start over and over.

X: The Time of Our Lives

Bengali Indian author Amitav Ghosh advances that climate change breaks up the distinction between the human and the natural. "What we see now," he contemplates, "is an environment, a nonhuman world, which is completely animated by human actions. It's the stuff we put into the atmosphere that is actually creating these incredible perturbations all around us, like Hurricane Sandy. They are not something that we could call 'natural.' They are something on which we have left our own fingerprints and they're coming back to visit us in these ways" (Paulson 2017). Ghosh speaks of animation by human action: the impact it will have on ever-growing numerosities of people. What does a landscape look like when it is simulated and enlivened by humans?

LatinX gives us a preview of this transitory state of being—the direction where bodies are moving—and the spaces they occupy. To understand the natural we must use, as well, the unnatural—or, as Ghosh has it, employ a language or retrace "something that we would call 'natural'"—something natural like.

Or maybe it is something like "Subject X," a matter referencing the perceiving subject that "owes nothing to what we otherwise know about the world" and that recreates and reconstitutes "the world at each moment" (Merleau-Ponti 2012, 214). LatinX is pointing us to an explicit direction, where climate change, climatological migrations, and LatinX human existence all bombard us. They are vital to the activation of a LatinXness falling in and out of the ongoing new starts in life that this contemporary moment demands.

The browning of the Earth and the browning of the population are asymptotically approaching each other. They may never need to touch, but these two things are manifesting a meeting space: they are planetary residue, a lens for 2050 from where we can see a natural world through LatinX subjectivity. LatinX does not eclipse anything. It emerged at the dawning of the twenty-first century, spreading to this abrupt present when Latina and Latino conventional ways of being no longer seem viable and extend to an X-ness of being where abstract notions of the unnatural are concretized so that we can begin to apprehend what the natural is. Or can be.

From the World Wide Web to the Webs of Life, LatinX links a subjectivity. X is our inseparable axis, our periodizing logic. The X of adaptation, of proximity: not so much of "a coming together *in* time, but *of* times" (Cox and Lund 2016, 11). X as the world that we live in, that we wait for, that we struggle for.

The X of the unexpected. Changing the course of life events. X on the fly. Transmundane X. X as an unknow-it-all. Marking what we can or cannot assimilate. X bodies of thought thinking the unthinkable (see Scranton 2018; Trouillot 1995).

X as a helix ushering in the methodologically experimental. LatinX research *of* and *in* the moment, revealing how and what we process today. X of writing, rewriting, and reflecting. Giving substance and texture to this analytic yet irresolvable exploration.

X as your trajectory.

X as ___.

Acknowledgments

With deep gratitude, I recognize my social network of dear and invaluable friends and colleagues for the conversations, time, encouragement, and kindnesses: Francisco-J. Hernández Adrián, Miguel Segovia, Gloria Chacón, Russell Contreras, Norman Holland, Marc Schachter, Priscilla Wald, Antonio Viego, Richard Rosa, Walter Mignolo, Roberto Dainotto, Michaeline Crichlow, Sarah Deutsch, Anna Krylova, María DeGuzmán, Tanya Shields, Kirsten Silva Gruesz, Arturo Arias, John Morán González, Raúl Coronado, Richard Perez, Belinda Rincón, Lázaro Lima, Rodrigo Lazo, Marissa K. López, Maria A. Windell, Benjamin J. Robertson, Rene Galvan, Jaime Acosta Gonzalez, and Dell Williams. A special mention to the Program in Latino/a Studies in the Global South and the Department of Romance Studies at Duke University for the institutional support. Many thanks, of course, to my editor, Danielle Kasprzak, for her generous attention and for believing in this project so early on. Heartfelt thanks—and more thanks—to Eduardo Contreras, my first and last reader, my sounding board, my most trusted interlocutor, my very best friend, my kindred spirit. Epic thanks to my pawsome teenager and forever baby, Theodor W. Adorno, my cherished catito, for always running to greet me no matter the hour, for being a devoted companion, for the love. Thank you all for the collective energy and for the parts you have played in making this work possible.

Works Cited

Acosta, Grisel Y. 2015. "Environmentalism." *The Routledge Companion to Latino/a Literature*, edited by Suzanne Bost and Frances R. Aparicio, 195–203. London: Routledge.

Adamson, Joni, and Scott Slovic, eds. 2009. "Ethnicity and Ecocriticism." *MELUS* 34, no. 2 (Summer).

Adler, Tamar. 2015. "Superstar Chef Enrique Olvera Will Change the Way You Think about Mexican Food." *Vogue*, June 30. http://www.vogue.com/13276858/chef-enrique-olvera-cosme-mexican-restaurant accessed December 31, 2016.

Agamben, Giorgio. 2009. *What Is an Apparatus?* Translated by David Kishik and Stefan Pedatella. Stanford, Calif.: Stanford University Press.

Agren, David. 2018. "Mexico Protesters Fear U.S.-Owned Brewery Will Drain Their Land Dry." *Guardian*, February 4. https://www.theguardian.com/world/2018/feb/04/mexico-water-brewery-mexicali-constellation-brands.

Aguirre, Robert D. 2005. *Informal Empire: Mexico and Central America in Victorian Culture*. Minneapolis: University of Minnesota Press.

Aldama, Frederick Luis, and Christopher González, eds. 2019. *Latinx Studies: The Key Concepts*. New York: Routledge.

Aldama, Frederick Luis, ed. 2016. *Latinx Comic Book Storytelling: An Odyssey by Interview*. San Diego, Calif.: Hyperbole Books.

Anderson, Jill and Nin Solis, eds. 2014. *Los Otros Dreamers*. Mexico City: Jill Anderson & Nin Solis.

Andréu, Tomás. 2014. "La sequía da paso un año más al fantasma del hambre." *El Faro*, September 8. https://elfaro.net/es/201409/noticias/15893/La-sequ%C3%ADa-da-paso-un-a%C3%B1o-m%C3%A1s-al-fantasma-del-hambre.htm, accessed December 12, 2017.

Appadurai, Arjun, ed. 1988. *The Social Life of Things: Commodities in Cultural Perspective*. Cambridge: Cambridge University Press.

Arias, Arturo. 2003. "Central American-Americans: Invisibility, Power, and Representation in the U.S. Latino World." *Latino Studies* 1, no. 1: 168–87.

Arias, Arturo, and Claudia Milian. 2013. "U.S. Central Americans: Representations, Agency, and Communities." *Latino Studies* 11, no. 2 (Summer): 131–49.

Basok, Tanya, Danièle Bélanger, Martha Luz Rojas Wiesner, and Guillermo Candiz. 2015. *Rethinking Transit Migration: Precarity, Mobility, and Self-Making in Mexico*. New York: Palgrave Macmillan.

Bawden, Tom. 2015. "Refugee Crisis: Is Climate Change Affecting Mass Migration?" *Independent*, September 7. http://www.independent.co.uk/news/world/refugee-crisis-is-climate-change-affecting-mass-migration-10490434.html, accessed December 9, 2017.

Beaubien, Jason. 2019. "Whatever Happened To . . . The Mysterious Kidney Disease Striking Central America?" NPR. 26 August. https://www.npr.org/sections/goatsandsoda/2019/08/26/753834371/whatever-happened-to-the-mysterious-kidney-disease-striking-central-america, accessed August 26, 2019.

Beeler, Carolyn. 2018. "How Do We Process Doom-and-Gloom Climate News? How Should We?" *PRI*, June 21. https://www.pri.org/stories/2018-06-21/how-do-we-process-doom-and-gloom-climate-news-how-should-we, accessed June 21, 2018.

Beltrán, Cristina. 2010. *The Trouble with Unity: Latino Politics and the Creation of Identity*. New York: Oxford University Press.

Benavides, Sofia. 2018. "¿Es machista el idioma español?: El debate sobre arrobas, equis y términos sexistas." *Infobae*, January 28. https://www.infobae.com/america/cultura-america/2018/01/27/es-machista-el-idioma-espanol-el-debate-sobre-arrobas-equis-y-terminos-sexistas/, accessed March 31, 2019.

Bhabha, Jacqueline. 2016. *Child Migration and Human Rights in a Global Age*. Princeton, N.J.: Princeton University Press.

Bilger, Wenzel, and Gabriela Rangel. 2014. "An Interview with Mark Dion." *Unity of Nature: Alexander von Humboldt and the Americas*. Bielefeld: Kerber Verlag.

Bogdan, Robert. 1988. *Freak Show: Presenting Human Oddities for Amusement and Profit*. Chicago, Ill.: University of Chicago Press.

Bolstad, Erika. 2017. "High Ground Is Becoming Hot Property as Sea Level Rises." *Scientific American*, May 1. https://www.scientificamerican.com/article/high-ground-is-becoming-hot-property-as-sea-level-rises/, accessed December 30, 2017.

Bonneuil, Christophe, and Jean-Baptiste Fressoz. 2015. *The Shock of the Anthropocene*. Translated by David Fernbach. London: Verso.

Bukatman, S. 1994. "X-Bodies (The Torment of the Mutant Superhero)." In *Uncontrollable Bodies: Testimonies of Identity and Culture,* edited by R. Sappington and T. Stallings, 93–129. Seattle, Wash.: Bay Press.

Butler, Bethonie. 2017. "It's Time to End the Tired Awards Show Jokes at Sofia Vergara's Expense." *Washington Post*, January 9. https://www.washingtonpost.com/news/arts-and-entertainment/wp/2017/01/09/its-time-to-end-the-tired-awards-show-jokes-at-sofia-vergaras-expense/?utm_term=.6820d7498b5f, accessed January 9, 2017.

Calma, Justine. 2017. "How New York City Is Tackling a Mental Health Crisis Spurred by Hurricane Sandy." *Grist*, December 20. http://grist .org/article/how-new-york-city-is-tackling-a-mental-health-crisis -spurred-by-hurricane-sandy/, accessed December 22, 2017.

Cammisa, Rebecca, dir. 2009. *Which Way Home*. Tarrytown: Documentress Films.

Carrillo, Socorro. 2016. "'Latinx Is Me': How One Letter Links Controversy, Community." *Cronkite News*, August 12. https:// cronkitenews.azpbs.org/2016/08/12/LatinX-one-letter-links -controversy-community/, accessed December 29, 2016.

Carson, Rachel. (1962) 2002. *Silent Spring*. Boston, Mass.: Houghton Mifflin. Reprint, Boston, Mass.: Mariner Books. Citations refer to the Mariner edition.

Casid, Jill H. 2018. "Necrolandscaping." In *Natura: Environmental Aesthetics after Landscape*, edited by Jens Andermann, Lisa Blackmore, and Dayron Carrillo Morrell, 237–64. Zurich: Diaphanes.

Castillo, Ana. 2014. *Massacre of the Dreamers: Essays on Xicanisma*. Albuquerque: University of New Mexico Press.

Chacón, Gloria Elizabeth. 2019. "Indian Trouble." *Cultural Dynamics* 31, nos. 1–2: 50–61.

Chandler, Nahum Dimitri. 2014. *X: The Problem of the Negro as a Problem for Thought*. New York: Fordham University Press.

Chavez, Nicole. 2017. "California Fire: Resident Says Neighborhood Looks like 'War Zone.'" CNN, December 18. http://www.cnn.com/2017/12/17 /us/california-fires/index.html, accessed December 18, 2017.

Chinchilla, Norma Stoltz, and Nora Hamilton. 2007. "Central America: Guatemala, Honduras, Nicaragua." In *The New Americans: A Guide to Immigration since 1965*, edited by Mary C. Waters, Reed Ueda, and Helen B. Marrow, 328–39. Cambridge, Mass.: Harvard University Press.

Cisneros, Sandra. 1984. *The House on Mango Street*. Houston, Tex.: Arte Público Press.

Cisneros, Sandra. 2019. "Puro Amor: A Conversation with Sandra Cisneros." The UNC Latina/o Studies Program at The University of North Carolina at Chapel Hill, February 20.

Contreras, Eduardo. 2019. *Latinos and the Liberal City: Politics and Protest in San Francisco*. Philadelphia: University of Pennsylvania Press.

Cordova, Cary. 2017. *The Heart of the Mission: Latino Art and Politics in San Francisco*. Philadelphia: University of Pennsylvania Press.

Cox, Geoff, and Jacob Lund. 2016. *The Contemporary Condition: Introductory Thoughts on Contemporaneity and Contemporary Art*. Berlin: Stemberg Press.

Danticat, Edwidge. 2019. "'All Geography Is within Me': Writing Beginnings, Life, Death, Freedom, and Salt." *World Literature Today*,

Winter. https://www.worldliteraturetoday.org/2019/winter/all
-geography-within-me-writing-beginnings-life-death-freedom-and
-salt-edwidge-danticat, accessed January 3, 2019.

Dávila, Arlene. 2001. *Latinos, Inc.: The Marketing and Making of a People*.
Berkeley: University of California Press.

Dawson, Ashley. 2017. *Extreme Cities: The Peril and Promise of Urban Life
in the Age of Climate Change*. London: Verso.

De Genova, Nicholas. 2017. "The Incorrigible Subject: Mobilizing a Critical
Geography of (Latin) America through the Autonomy of Migration."
Journal of Latin American Geography 16, no. 1 (April): 17–42.

De Genova, Nicholas, and Ana Yolanda Ramos-Zayas. 2003. *Latino
Crossings: Mexicans, Puerto Ricans, and the Politics of Race and
Citizenship*. New York: Routledge.

del Rincón, Beatriz. 2015. "Sequía en Centroamérica: una crisis
silenciosa." Eldiario.es, July 30. http://www.eldiario.es/ayudaenaccion
/Centroamerica-sequia-crisis_6_414768531.html, accessed December
10, 2017.

Derrida, Jacques. 2007. *Learning to Live Finally: The Last Interview*.
Translated by Pascale-Anne Brault and Michael Naas. Hoboken, N.J.:
Melville House.

Dibble, Sandra. 2018. "A Battle over a U.S. Brewery in Mexicali." *San Diego
Union-Tribune*, January 29. http://www.sandiegouniontribune.com
/news/border-baja-california/sd-me-constellation-mexicali-20180126
-story.html, accessed February 12, 2018.

EFE. 2019. "La igualdad se defiende con la 'e' de 'todes' en Argentina." *El
Universal*, January 26. https://www.eluniversal.com.mx/cultura/letras
/la-igualdad-se-defiende-con-e-de-todes-en-argentina, accessed
March 31, 2019.

"The 11 Cities Most Likely to Run out of Drinking Water—like Cape
Town." 2018. *BBC*. February 11. http://www.bbc.com/news/world
-42982959, accessed February 11, 2018.

Erickson, Amanda. 2017. "The U.S. Has More Climate Skeptics than
Anywhere Else on Earth. Blame the GOP." *Washington Post*, November
17. https://www.washingtonpost.com/news/worldviews/wp/2017/11
/17/the-u-s-has-more-climate-skeptics-than-anywhere-else-on-earth
-blame-the-gop/?utm_term=.a233d7344d53, accessed November 19,
2017.

Fernandes, Deepa. 2018. "With Kids' Health Suffering, One Guatemalan
Town Is Trying to Adapt to Climate Change." *PRI*, January 23. https://
www.pri.org/stories/2018-01-23/kids-health-suffered-one-guatemalan
-town-trying-adapt-climate-change, accessed January 23, 2018.

Fernández, Lilia. 2012. *Brown in the Windy City: Mexicans and Puerto
Ricans in Postwar Chicago*. Chicago, Ill.: University of Chicago Press.

Fichter, Angela. 2017. "Puerto Rico's Mental Health Crisis Is an American

Disaster." *Grist*, December. http://grist.org/article/puerto-ricos
-mental-health-crisis-is-an-american-disaster/, accessed December 22,
2017.

Fiol-Matta, Licia, and Macarena Gómez-Barris. 2014. "Introduction: *Las
Américas Quarterly*." *American Quarterly* 66, no. 3 (Summer): 493–504.

Food and Agriculture Organization of the United Nations (FAO). N.d.
"Drought in the Dry Corridor of Central America." http://www.fao.org
/emergencies/crisis/dry-corridor/en/, accessed December 9, 2017.

Food and Agriculture Organization of the United Nations (FAO). 2016.
"Dry Corridor: Central America." *Situation Report*, June. http://www
.fao.org/3/a-br092e.pdf.

Forero, Juan. 2001. "Medellín Journal: A Coffee Icon Rides His Mule Off
into the Sunset." *New York Times*, November 24. http://www.nytimes
.com/2001/11/24/world/medellin-journal-a-coffee-icon-rides-his
-mule-off-into-the-sunset.html, accessed January 20, 2017.

Franklin, Sarah. 2013. *Biological Relatives: IVF, Stem Cells, and the Future
of Kinship*. Durham, N.C.: Duke University Press.

Fukunaga, Cary Joji, dir. 2009. *Sin Nombre*. New York: NBC Universal.

Funes, Yessenia. 2017. "Ever Wondered What 'Latinx' Means? This Video
Will Explain." *ColorLines*, April 3. https://www.colorlines.com/articles
/watch-ever-wondered-what-latinx-means-video-will-explain,
accessed April 3, 2017.

Galeano, Eduardo. 2002. "An SOS from the South." *Guardian*, August
22. https://www.theguardian.com/environment/2002/aug/22
/worldsummit2002.earth19, accessed December 10, 2017.

Galton, Francis. 1884. *Record of Family Faculties*. London: Macmillan.

Galvan, R. 2017. "EE/UU: Exquisite Expression/Unsettling Utterance."
Cultural Dynamics 29, no. 3 (August): 186–92.

Gear, Elizabeth Sulis. 2017. "The Forgotten History of the Koreans
of Mexico and Cuba." *Feature Shoot*, February 14. http://www
.featureshoot.com/2017/02/forgotten-history-koreans-mexico-cuba,
accessed March 30, 2017.

Ghosh, Amitav. 2016. *The Great Derangement: Climate Change and the
Unthinkable*. Chicago, Ill.: The University of Chicago Press.

Gilberto, Bebel. 2018. Music Concert. Durham, N.C.: Motorco Music Hall,
February 15.

Goldstein, Dana. 2016. "America: This Is Your Future." *Politico*, November
30. https://www.politico.com/agenda/story/2016/11/political-future-of
-america-generations-diversity-tensions-000235, accessed November
19, 2017.

Goodell, Jeff. 2017. "The Year Is 2037. This Is What Happens When
the Hurricane Hits Miami." *Guardian*, December 17. https://www
.theguardian.com/us-news/2017/dec/17/miami-hurricane-2037
-climate-change, accessed December 17, 2017.

Goodman, Amy. 2017. "Mexican Writer Valeria Luiselli on Child Refugees
    and Rethinking the Language around Immigration." *Democracy Now*,
    April 18. https://www.democracynow.org/2017/4/18/mexican_writer
    _valeria_luiselli_on_child, accessed April 18, 2017.

Gordon, Ian. 2014. "70,000 Kids Will Show Up Alone at Our Border This
    Year: What Happens to Them?" *Mother Jones*, (July–August). http://
    www.motherjones.com/politics/2014/06/child-migrants-surge
    -unaccompanied-central-america, accessed March 30, 2017.

Graeber, David. 2011. *Revolutions in Reverse: Essays on Politics, Violence,
    Art, and Imagination*. London: Minor Compositions.

Grathwohl, Casper. 2017. "Youthquake: Behind the Scenes on Selecting
    the Word of the Year." *Oxford Dictionaries*, December 14. https://blog
    .oxforddictionaries.com/2017/12/14/youthquake-word-of-the-year
    -2017-commentary/?__prclt=XM6PW1vI, accessed December 22, 2017.

"Greater Mexico and U.S. Latinx Perspectives, Open Rank Faculty Cluster
    Hire 2016–17, University of California, Riverside." 2016. *Chronicle
    of Higher Education*, December 14. https://chroniclevitae.com/jobs
    /0000347286-01.

Grossman, Edith. 2010. *Why Translation Matters*. New Haven, Conn.: Yale
    University Press.

Gruesz, Kirsten Silva. 2006. "The Gulf of Mexico System and the
    'Latinness' of New Orleans." *American Literary History* 18, no. 3 (Fall):
    468–95.

Gutierrez, Sandra. 2011. *The New Southern-Latino Table: Recipes that
    Bring Together the Bold and Beloved Flavors of Latin America and the
    American South*. Chapel Hill, N.C.: The University of North Carolina
    Press.

Gutierrez, Sandra. 2016. "A Voice from the Nuevo South." *Oxford
    American*, October 11. http://www.oxfordamerican.org/item/977-a
    -voice-from-the-nuevo-south, accessed December 28, 2016.

Halley, Catherine. 2018. "On the Side of Climate Solutions: An Interview
    with Paul Lussier." *JSTOR Daily*, February 7. https://daily.jstor.org/side
    -climate-solutions-interview-paul-lussier/, accessed February 7, 2018.

Hartog, François. 2015. *Regimes of Historicity: Presentism and Experiences
    of Time*. Translated by Saskia Brown. New York: Columbia University
    Press.

Harvard University YouTube Channel. 2012. "Travelers in Hiding:
    Telling a Story of Central Americans in Mexico/Radcliffe Institute."
    YouTube video, November 20. https://www.youtube.com/watch?v=
    BpwnjYqbqDI, accessed April 7, 2014.

Hernández Cruz, Victor. 2017. *Beneath the Spanish*. Minneapolis, Minn.:
    Coffee House Press.

Holpuch, Amanda. 2017. "Despair and Anxiety: Puerto Rico's 'Living
    Emergency' as a Mental Health Crisis Unfolds." *Guardian*, August

7. https://www.theguardian.com/world/2018/aug/07/despair-and
-anxiety-puerto-ricos-living-emergency-as-a-mental-health-crisis
-unfolds, accessed August 7, 2018.

Holthaus, Eric. 2017. "Let It Go: The Arctic Will Never Be Frozen Again."
Grist, December 18. http://grist.org/article/let-it-go-the-arctic-will
-never-be-frozen-again/, accessed December 18, 2017.

Hondagneu-Sotelo, Pierrette. 2007. *Doméstica: Immigrant Workers
Cleaning and Caring in the Shadows of Affluence*. Berkeley: University of
California Press.

Horan, Elizabeth. 2004. "Susana Chávez-Silverman's *Killer Crónicas:
Urbane Gardens of Earthly Delight*." *Feministas Unidas* 24, no. 2 (Fall):
25–26.

Igo, Sarah Elizabeth. 2007. *The Averaged American: Surveys, Citizens, and
the Making of a Mass Public*. Cambridge, Mass.: Harvard University Press.

Inan, Ilhan. 2012. *The Philosophy of Curiosity*. New York: Routledge.

Inocéncio, Josh. 2017. "Why I Won't Use Latinx." *Spectrum South*,
September 6. https://www.spectrumsouth.com/wont-use-latinx/,
accessed November 6, 2018.

Itäranta, Emmi. 2014. *Memory of Water*. New York: Harper Collins.

Jackson Stephen T., ed. 2009. *Essay on the Geography of Plants: Alexander
von Humboldt and Aimé Bonpland*. Translated by Sylvie Romanowski.
Chicago, Ill.: The University of Chicago Press.

Jamal, Urooba. 2017. "'Fuck the Binary!': How 'Latinx' Reimagines Gender
Inclusivity." teleSur, May 17. http://www.telesurtv.net/english/opinion
/Fuck-the-Binary-How-Latinx-Reimagines-Gender-Inclusivity
-20170517-0010.html, accessed May 17, 2017.

Jenner, Frances. 2018. "Opinion: Todos Todas y Todes: The New Trend
of a Genderless Spanish Is Sparking Debate across the Continent."
Argentine Reports, June 20. https://argentinareports.com/opinion
-genderless-spanish/1171/, accessed March 31, 2019.

Jones, Grace. 2015. *I'll Never Write My Memoirs*. New York: Gallery Books.

Kindley, Evan. 2016. *Questionnaire*. New York: Bloomsbury.

Krogstad, Jens Manuel. 2014. "With Fewer New Arrivals, Census Lowers
Hispanic Population Projections." Pew Research Center, December 16.
http://www.pewresearch.org/fact-tank/2014/12/16/with-fewer-new
-arrivals-census-lowers-hispanic-population-projections-2/, accessed
November 19, 2017.

Lakhani, Nina. 2016. "'Time Was Running Out': Honduran Activist's
Last Days Marked by Threats." *Guardian*, April 25. https://www
.theguardian.com/global-development/2016/apr/25/berta-caceres
-murder-honduras-death-threats-hitman-agua-zarca-dam, accessed
December 31, 2017.

Latino USA. 2016. "Latinx: The Ungendering of the Spanish Language."
National Public Radio podcast, January 29. http://www.npr.org/2016

/01/29/464886588/latinx-the-ungendering-of-the-spanish-language, accessed January 22, 2017.

Lear, Linda. 2002. Introduction to *Silent Spring* by Rachel Carson, x-xix. Boston, Mass.: Mariner Books.

Lefebvre, Henri. 1992. *The Production of Space*. Malden, Mass.: Wiley-Blackwell.

Leguizamo, John. 2007. *Pimps, Hos, Playa Hatas, and All the Rest of My Hollywood Friends: My Life*. New York: Harper.

Leiva, Noé. 2015. "Campesinos hondureños pasan hambre por la sequía." *El Faro*, August 1. https://elfaro.net/es/201507/internacionales/17241/Campesinos-hondure%C3%B1os-pasan-hambre-por-la-sequ%C3%ADa.htm, accessed December 12, 2017.

Leutert, Stephanie. 2018. "How Climate Change Is Affecting Rural Honduras and Pushing People North." *Washington Post*, November 6. https://www.washingtonpost.com/news/global-opinions/wp/2018/11/06/how-climate-change-is-affecting-rural-honduras-and-pushing-people-north/?utm_term=.bf02b562d908, accessed November 6, 2018.

Logue, Josh. 2015. "Latina/o/x." *Inside Higher Ed*, December 8. https://www.insidehighered.com/news/2015/12/08/students-adopt-gender-nonspecific-term-Latinx-be-more-inclusive, accessed December 29, 2016.

Luiselli, Valeria. 2017. *Tell Me How It Ends: An Essay in Forty Questions*. Minneapolis, Minn.: Coffee House Press.

Maclachlan, Ian. 2012. "Global Consumption Patterns." *21st Century Geography: A Reference Handbook*, edited by Joseph P. Stoltman, 399–410. Thousand Oaks, Calif.: Sage Publications.

Maloney, Devon. 2014. "Our Obsession with Online Quizzes Comes from Fear, Not Narcissism." *Wired*, March 6. https://www.wired.com/2014/03/buzzfeed-quizzes, accessed April 23, 2017.

Manz, Olivia. 2014. "Freshmen Buy Same Jacket, Discover Same Genes." *Tulane Hullaballoo*, January 16. http://www.tulanehullabaloo.com/news/freshmen-buy-same-jacket-discover-same-genes-1.3130636#.UuBQXrQo7cu, accessed January 22, 2014.

Markham, Lauren. 2017. *The Far Away Brothers: Two Young Migrants and the Making of an American Life*. New York: Crown.

Markham, Lauren. 2018. "A Warming World Creates Desperate People." *New York Times*, June 29. https://www.nytimes.com/2018/06/29/opinion/sunday/immigration-climate-change-trump.html, accessed July 22, 2018.

Markon, Jerry. 2016. "Former Judges Challenge Official Who Said 3-Year-Olds Can Represent Selves in Immigration Court." *Washington Post*, March 15. https://www.washingtonpost.com/world/national-security/former-judges-challenge-official-who-said-three-year-olds-can-represent-themselves-in-immigration-court/2016/03/15/d9cb0538

-eaaf-11e5-b0fd-073d5930a7b7_story.html?utm_term=.ac101c88e78e, accessed May 2, 2017.

Marshall, Tim. 2015. *Prisoners of Geography: Ten Maps That Explain Everything about the World*. New York: Scribner.

Marti, Diana. 2018. *"Latinx Now!* First Look: See the Promo for E! News and Telemundo's New Show." Eonline, October 1. https://www.eonline .com/news/972872/latinx-now-first-look-see-the-promo-for-e-news -and-telemundo-s-new-show, accessed October 17, 2018.

Martínez, Óscar. 2013. *The Beast: Riding the Rails and Dodging Narcos on the Migrant Trail*. Translated by Daniela Maria Ugaz and John Washington. London: Verso.

Martínez, Óscar. 2014. "Los niños no se van: Se los llevan." *ElFaro*, July 13. https://elfaro.net/es/201407/noticias/15683/Los-ni%C3%B1os-no-se -van-se-los-llevan.htm, accessed May 13, 2017.

Martínez, Óscar. 2016. *A History of Violence: Living and Dying in Central America*. New York: Verso.

Medek, Danielle E., Joel Schwartz, and Samuel S. Myer. 2017. "Estimated Effects of Future Atmospheric CO2 Concentrations on Protein Intake and the Risk of Protein Deficiency by Country and Region." *Environmental Health Perspectives*, August. https://ehp.niehs.nih.gov /EHP41/, accessed May 21, 2018.

Mentz, Steve. "Brown." 2013. *Prismatic Ecology: Ecotheory beyond Green*. Edited by Jeffrey Jerome Cohen, 193–212. Minneapolis: University of Minnesota Press.

Merleau-Ponty, Maurice. 2012. *Phenomenology of Perception*. Translated by Donald A. Landes. New York: Routledge.

Merriman, Helena. 2016. "Why Are 10,000 Migrant Children Missing in Europe?" BBC, October 12. https://www.bbc.com/news/world-europe -37617234, accessed October 12, 2016.

Meyer, Robinson. 2015. "What Is Fusion? The Millennial-Targeted News Site Is 'Pressing the Start Button' Tuesday." *Atlantic*, February 3. https://www.theatlantic.com/technology/archive/2015/02/what-is -fusion/385112/, accessed April 17, 2017.

Milian, Claudia. 2013. *Latining America: Black-Brown Passages and the Coloring of Latino/a Studies*. Athens: University of Georgia Press.

Milian, Claudia. 2016. "Latin." *Keywords for Southern Studies*. Edited by Scott Romine and Jennifer Rae Greeson, 179–88. Athens: University of Georgia Press.

Milian, Claudia, ed. 2017. "Theorizing LatinX." *Cultural Dynamics* 29, no. 3 (August).

Milian, Claudia, ed. 2019. "LatinX Studies: Variations and Velocities." *Cultural Dynamics* 31, nos. 1–2 (February–May).

Miller, Todd. 2017. *Storming the Wall: Climate Change, Migration, and Homeland Security*. San Francisco: City Lights.

Milman, Oliver, Emily Holden, and David Agren. 2018. "The Unseen Driver behind the Migrant Caravan: Climate Change." *Guardian*, October 30. https://www.theguardian.com/world/2018/oct/30 /migrant-caravan-causes-climate-change-central-america, accessed October 39, 2018.

Mitchell, Sally. 1996. *Daily Life in Victorian England*. Westport, Conn.: Greenwood.

Molina, Moisés. 2012. "La X en la frente. ¿Por qué 'la X en la frente?'" SDPnoticias, December 28. http://www.sdpnoticias.com/columnas /2012/12/28/la-xen-la-frente-por-que-la-x-en-la-frente, accessed January 8, 2017.

Moore, Jason W. 2015. *Capitalism in the Web of Life: Ecology and the Accumulation of Capital*. London: Verso.

Mora, Cristina. 2014. *Making Hispanics: How Activists, Bureaucrats, and Media Constructed a New American*. Chicago, Ill.: University of Chicago Press.

Moraga, Cherríe. 2011. *A Xicana Codex of Changing Consciousness, 2000– 2010*. Durham, N.C.: Duke University Press.

Morales, Ed. 2018a. *Latinx: The New Force of American Politics*. New York: Verso.

Morales, Ed. 2018b. "Why I Embrace the Term Latinx." *Guardian*, January 8. https://www.theguardian.com/commentisfree/2018/jan/08/why-i -embrace-the-term-latinx, accessed January 8, 2018.

Morton, Margaret. 2016. "The Future of the Arts Is Latinx: Q&A with Artist Teresita Fernandez." Ford Foundation, September 26. https:// www.fordfoundation.org/ideas/equals-change-blog/posts/the-future -of-the-arts-is-latinx-qa-with-artist-teresita-fernandez/, accessed January 15, 2017.

Moore, Terry. 2012. "Why Is 'X' the Unknown?" TED, February. https:// www.ted.com/talks/terry_moore_why_is_x_the_unknown#t-2593, accessed September 29, 2018.

Muñoz, José Esteban. 2009. *Cruising Utopia: The Then and There of Queer Futurity*. New York: New York University Press.

Nail, Thomas. 2015. *The Figure of the Migrant*. Stanford, Calif.: Stanford University Press.

Nazario, Sonia. 2002. "Enrique's Journey: A Six-Part Times Series." *Los Angeles Times*, September 29. https://www.latimes.com/nation /immigration/la-fg-enriques-journey-sg-storygallery.html, accessed September 27, 2018.

Nazario, Sonia. 2007. *Enrique's Journey: The Story of a Boy's Dangerous Odyssey to Reunite with His Mother*. New York: Random House.

Ngai, Mae M. 2004. *Impossible Subjects: Illegal Aliens and the Making of Modern America*. Princeton, N.J.: Princeton University Press.

Nixon, Rob. 2013. *Slow Violence and the Environmentalism of the Poor*. Cambridge, Mass.: Harvard University Press.

Norgaard, Kari Marie. 2011. *Living in Denial: Climate Change, Emotions, and Everyday Life*. Cambridge, Mass.: MIT Press.

Nuño-Pérez, Stephen, and Gwen Aviles. 2019. "Is 'Latinx' Elitist? Some Push Back at the Word's Growing Use." NBC News, March 7. https:// www.nbcnews.com/news/latino/latinx-elitist-some-push-back-word -s-growing-use-n957036, accessed March 7, 2019.

Oboler, Suzanne. 1995. *Ethnic Labels, Latino Lives: Identity and the Politics of (Re)Presentation in the United States*. Minneapolis: University of Minnesota Press.

Okihiro, Gary Y. 2016. *Third World Studies: Theorizing Liberation*. Durham, N.C.: Duke University Press.

Onishi, Norimitsu, and Somini Sengupta. 2018. "Dangerously Low on Water, Cape Town Now Faces 'Day Zero.'" *New York Times*, January 30. https://www.nytimes.com/2018/01/30/world/africa/cape-town -day-zero.html, accessed January 30, 2018.

Ortiz, Paul. 2018. *An African American and Latinx History of the United States*. Boston, Mass.: Beacon Press.

Ortiz, Ricardo. 2019. *Latinx Literature Now: Between Evanescence and Event*. New York: Palgrave Macmillan.

PBS NewsHour. 2018. "The 'Silent Massacre' Killing El Salvador's Sugarcane Workers." PBS, February 28. https://www.pbs.org /newshour/show/the-silent-massacre-killing-el-salvadors-sugarcane -workers, accessed March 1, 2018.

Padilla, Yesenia. 2016. "What Does 'Latinx' Mean? A Look at the Term That's Challenging Gender Norms." *Complex*, April 18. http://www .complex.com/life/2016/04/latinx/, accessed January 22, 2017.

Painter, Nell. 2018. *Old in Art School*. Berkeley, Calif.: Counterpoint.

Palencia, Gustavo. 2014. "Drought Leaves up to 2.81 Mln Hungry in Central America -U.N." Reuters, August 29. https://af.reuters.com /article/commodities07News/idAFL1N0QZ2O420140829, accessed December 9, 2017.

Palmer, Jane. 2017. "Climate Change Is Turning Dehydration into a Deadly Epidemic." *JSTOR Daily*, September 7. https://daily.jstor.org /climate-change-dehydration-deadly-epidemic/, accessed December 10, 2017.

Paredes, Américo. 1989. *George Washington Gómez: A Mexicotexan Novel*. Houston, Tex.: Arte Público Press.

Pastrana, Antonio (Jay), Juan Battle, and Angelique Harris. 2017. *An Examination of Latinx LGBT Populations across the United States: Intersections of Race and Sexuality*. New York: Palgrave Macmillan.

Patel, Raj, and Jason W. Moore. 2017. *A History of the World in Seven Cheap Things*. Berkeley: University of California Press.

Paulson, Steve. 2017. "Where's the Great 'Climate Change Novel'? A Conversation with Amitav Ghosh." *Los Angeles Review of Books*,

September 22. https://lareviewofbooks.org/article/wheres-the
-great-climate-change-novel-a-conversation-with-amitav-ghosh/#!,
accessed January 1, 2018.

Pelaez Lopez, Alan. 2018. "The X in Latinx Is a Wound, Not a Trend."
EFNIKS, September 13. http://efniks.com/the-deep-dive-pages/2018/9
/11/the-x-in-latinx-is-a-wound-not-a-trend, accessed September 15, 2018.

Peña, Fátima. 2016. "Los pobres aguantan más hambre cuando llega El
Niño." *El Faro*, July 3. https://elfaro.net/es/201607/el_salvador/18595
/Los-pobres-aguantan-m%C3%A1s-hambre-cuando-llega-El-Ni%C3
%B1o.htm, accessed December 12, 2017.

Perez D., Sonia. 2019. "After Crossing into Guatemala, Migrants Set Sights
on Mexico." Associated Press, January 16. https://www.apnews.com
/8d61ce90f56d481fa2e3d90fd2b100ef, accessed January 16, 2019.

Popkin, Nathaniel. 2017. "Translating This Broken World: How to Tell
a Refugee's Story." *Literary Hub*, April 26. https://www.lithub.com
/translating-this-broken-world-how-to-tell-a-refugees-story, accessed
April 26, 2017.

Powers, John. 2017. "'Tell Me How It Ends' Offers a Moving, Humane
Portrait of Child Migrants." NPR, April 6. https://www.npr.org/2017
/04/06/521791352/tell-me-how-it-ends-offers-a-moving-humane
-portrait-of-child-migrants, accessed April 6, 2017.

Quintero, Adrianna, and Juanita Constible. 2016. "Nuestro Futuro:
Climate Change and U.S. Latinos." Nrdc, October 13. https://www
.nrdc.org/resources/nuestro-futuro-climate-change-and-us-latinos,
accessed December 17, 2017.

Ramirez, Tanisha Love, and Zeba Blay. 2016. "Why People Are
Using the Term 'Latinx.'" *Huffington Post*, July 5. https://www
.huffingtonpost.com/entry/why-people-are-using-the-term-latinx_us
_57753328e4b0cc0fa136a159, accessed July 5, 2016.

Ramirez-Rubio, Oriana, Michael D. McClean, Juan José Amador, and
Daniel R. Brooks. 2013. "An Epidemic of Chronic Kidney Disease
in Central America: An Overview." *Journal of Epidemiology and
Community Health* 67, no. 1 (January): 1–3.

Randewich, Noel, and Peter Henderson. 2017. "Latino Workers Flee
California Wine Country Fires for Shelters, Beaches." Reuters, October
14. https://www.reuters.com/article/us-california-fire-latinos/latino
-workers-flee-california-wine-country-fires-for-shelters-beaches
-idUSKBN1CJ0CJ, accessed December 18, 2017.

Rebok, Sandra. 2014. *Humboldt and Jefferson: A Transatlantic Friendship
of the Enlightenment*. Charlottesville: University of Virginia Press.

Reckdahl, Katy. 2014. "Genes that Fit: Tulane Freshmen Discover Shared
Sperm-Donor Dad." *New Orleans Advocate*, January 22. http://www
.theneworleansadvocate.com/home/8161964-172/genes-that-fit-tulane
-freshmen, accessed January 22, 2014.

Reichard, Raquel. 2015. "Why We Say Latinx: Trans and Gender Non-Conforming People Explain." *Latina*, August 29. http://www.latina.com/lifestyle/our-issues/why-we-say-LatinX-trans-gender-non-conforming-people-explain, accessed December 4, 2016.

Reuters Staff. 2016. "El Salvador Declares Drought Emergency for First Time Ever." Reuters, April 14. https://www.reuters.com/article/us-el-salvador-drought/el-salvador-declares-drought-emergency-for-first-time-ever-idUSKCN0XB2YM?TB_iframe=true&width=921.6&height=921.6, accessed December 9, 2017.

Reyes, Alfonso. 1993. *La X en la frente: textos sobre México*. México, D.F.: Universidad Nacional Autónoma de México.

Rivas, Jorge. 2017. "What We Mean When We Say Latinx." *Fusion*, April 13. http://fusion.net/what-we-mean-when-we-say-latinx-1794092929, accessed April 17, 2017.

Rivera, Fredo. 2019. "Precarity and Excess in the Latinopolis: Miami as Erzulie." *Cultural Dynamics* 31, nos. 1–2: 62–80.

Robbins, Gary. 2018. "'Latinos' Is Out, 'Latinx' Is In at UC San Diego in Nod to Evolving Gender and Sexuality Terms." *Los Angeles Times*, December 2. https://www.latimes.com/local/lanow/la-me-latino-latinx-ucsd-20181202-story.html, accessed December 2, 2018.

Robertson, Craig. 2010. *The Passport in America: The History of a Document*. Oxford: Oxford University Press.

Rodriguez, Ralph E. 2018. *Latinx Literature Unbound: Undoing Ethnic Expectation*. New York: Fordham University Press.

Rodríguez, Roberto. 1996. *The X in La Raza: An Anti-Book*. Albuquerque, N. Mex.: Roberto Rodríguez.

Roitman, Janet. 2014. *Anti-Crisis*. Durham, N.C.: Duke University Press.

Rosales, Arturo F. 1997. *Chicano! The History of the Mexican American Civil Rights Movement*. Houston, Tex.: Arte Público Press.

Royal Spanish Academy (@RAEinforma). Twitter Post. January 22, 2018, 11:32 PM. https://twitter.com/RAEinforma/status/955704857138225157, accessed March 31, 2019.

Ruiz, Iris D., and Raúl Sánchez, eds. 2016. *Decolonizing Rhetoric and Composition Studies: New Latinx Keywords for Theory and Pedagogy*. New York: Palgrave Macmillan.

Said, Edward W. 1975. *Beginnings: Intention and Method*. New York: Basic.

Sandoval-García, Carlos. 2017. *Exclusion and Forced Migration in Central America: No More Walls*. Translated by Kari Meyers. New York: Palgrave Macmillan.

Sassen, Saskia. 2014. *Expulsions: Brutality and Complexity in the Global Economy*. Cambridge, Mass.: Harvard University Press.

Sassen, Saskia. 2016. "A Massive Loss of Habitat: New Drivers for Migration." *Sociology of Development 2*, no. 2: 204–33.

Sassen, Saskia, and Giulia Torino. 2017. "Age of Extraction: An Interview

with Saskia Sassen." *King's Review*, November 24. http://kingsreview
.co.uk/articles/interview-saskia-sassen/, accessed December 28, 2017.

Schaub, Michael. 2018. "'Latinx,' 'Hangry' and 840 More Words Added
to the *Merriam-Webster Dictionary*." *Los Angeles Times*, September 4.
http://www.latimes.com/books/la-et-jc-lantinx-dictionary-20180904
-story.html, accessed September 4, 2018.

Schouten, Cory. 2017. "'Climate Gentrification' Could Add Value to
Elevation in Real Estate." CBS News, December 28. https://www
.cbsnews.com/news/climate-gentrification-home-values-rising-sea
-level/, accessed December 29, 2017.

Scranton, Roy. 2015. *Learning to Die in the Anthropocene: Reflections on the
End of Civilization*. San Francisco, Calif.: City Lights Books.

Scranton, Roy. 2018. *We're Doomed. Now What? Essays on War and Climate
Change*. New York: Soho Press.

Sellnow, Timothy L., and Matthew W. Seeger. 2013. *Theorizing Crisis
Communication*. Malden, Mass.: Wiley-Blackwell.

Semple, Kirk. 2018. "Young Migrants' Return to Mexico Is More 'Exile'
than Homecoming." *New York Times*, March 24. https://www
.nytimes.com/2018/03/24/world/americas/mexico-daca-dreamers
-immigration.html, accessed March 24, 2018.

Skyhorse, Brando. 2014. *Take This Man: A Memoir*. New York: Simon &
Schuster.

Smyth, Diane. 2019. "Contemporary Identity at Mundo Latinx." *British
Journal of Photography*, January 28. https://www.bjp-online.com/2019
/01/mundo-latinx/, accessed January 28, 2019.

Solnit, Rebecca. 2005. *A Field Guide to Getting Lost*. New York: Viking.

Sotomayor, Sonia. 2013. *My Beloved World*. New York: Alfred A. Knopf.

Spillers, Hortense J. 1987. "Mama's Baby, Papa's Maybe: An American
Grammar Book." *diacritics* 17, no. 2: 65–81.

St. Clair, Kassia. 2016. *The Secret Lives of Color*. New York: Penguin Books.

"Starbucking—Winter Appears on Your Morning on CN8." 2007. YouTube
video, February 8. https://www.youtube.com/watch?v=Ah75uC-s0vo,
accessed January 1, 2017.

Stasio, Frank. 2019. *The State of Things*. February 20. http://www.wunc
.org/post/writer-sandra-cisneros-documenting-unheard-nc-voices,
accessed January 8, 2017.

Tangeman, Bill, dir. 2007. *Starbucking*. Park City: Heretic Films. http://
www.starbuckseverywhere.net/.

Taylor, Paul, and D'vera Cohn. 2012. "A Milestone En Route to a Majority
Minority Nation." Pew Social Trends, November 7. http://www
.pewsocialtrends.org/2012/11/07/a-milestone-en-route-to-a-majority
-minority-nation/, accessed November 19, 2017.

teleSUR. 2018. "'Boycott Modelo Beer!' Mexicali Resiste Fights for Water
Rights." February 13. https://www.telesurtv.net/english/analysis

/Mexicali-Resiste-boycotts-Constellation-Brands-Grupo-Modelo
-20180213-0009.html, accessed February 13, 2018.

Terrio, Susan J. 2015. *Whose Child Am I? Unaccompanied, Undocumented Children in U.S. Immigration Custody.* Berkeley: University of California Press.

Thomas, Lorrin. 2010. *Puerto Rican Citizen: History and Political Identity in Twentieth-Century New York City.* Chicago, Ill.: University of Chicago Press.

The University of North Carolina Press. 2011. "Author Q&A." http:// uncpress.unc.edu/browse/author_interview?title_id=2217, accessed December 30, 2016.

Toomey, Diane. 2014. "Where Will Earth Head after Its 'Climate Departure'?" *YaleEnvironment360*, July 2. http://e360.yale.edu /features/interview_camilo_mora_where_will_earth_head_after_its _climate_departure, accessed December 11, 2017.

Toomey, Diane. 2016. "The Legacy of the Man Who Changed Our View of Nature." *YaleEnvironment360*, December 21. https://e360.yale.edu /features/legacy_of_the_man_who_change_our_view_of_nature _alexander_von_humboldt_andrea_wulf, accessed June 8, 2018.

Torpey, John. 2000. *The Invention of the Passport: Surveillance, Citizenship, and the State.* Cambridge: Cambridge University Press.

Torres, Lourdes. 2018. "Latinx." *Latino Studies* 16, no. 3 (October): 283–85.

Treviño, Jesus Salvador. 2001. *Eyewitness: A Filmmaker's Memoir of the Chicano Movement.* Houston, Tex.: Arte Público Press.

Trouillot, Michel-Rolph.1995. *Silencing the Past: Power and the Production of History.* Boston, Mass.: Beacon Press.

The University of North Carolina Press. 2011. "Author Q&A." http:// uncpress.unc.edu/browse/author_interview?title_id=2217, accessed December 30, 2016.

Valentine, Leonica, and Lorena Mongelli. 2013. "Man Finds $1M Lotto Winner in Hurricane Sandy Leaves." *New York Post*, December 27. https://nypost.com/2013/12/27/landscaper-finds-1m-lottery-winner -while-raking-hurricane-sandy-leaves/, accessed January 1, 2018.

Vazquez, Alexandra T. 2016. "The Mega Mezclapolis." In *Nonstop Metropolis: A New York City Atlas*, edited by Rebecca Solnit and Joshua Jelly-Schapiro, 111–18. Berkeley: University of California Press.

Velasco, Juan. 1996. "The 'X' in Race and Gender: Rethinking Chicano/a Cultural Production through the Paradigms of Xicanisma and Me(x) icanness." *The Americas Review* 24, no. 3–4: 218–30.

Viego, Antonio. 2017. "LatinX and the Neurologization of Self." *Cultural Dynamics* 29, no. 3 (August): 160–76.

Visram, Talib. 2018. "Colombia and Honduras Lead the Way in Tackling Devastating Coffee Rust Disease." CNN, August 8. https://money.cnn .com/2018/08/08/news/world/coffee-rust-honduras-colombia/index .html, accessed February 23, 2019.

Vonnegut, Kurt. 1994. "Speech to Class of 1994: Syracuse University Commencement." May 8. http://versailles1.tripod.com/syracuse.html, accessed December 28, 2016.

Wadhams, Peter. 2017. *A Farewell to Ice: A Report from the Arctic*. New York: Oxford University Press.

Wald, Sarah D., David J. Vázquez, Priscilla Solis Ybarra, and Sarah Jaquette Ray, eds. Forthcoming. *Latinx Environmentalisms: Place, Justice, and the Decolonial*. Philadelphia, Penn.: Temple University Press.

Washington, John, and Tracie Williams. 2018. "Portraits from The Exodus." *The Nation*, December 14. https://www.thenation.com/article /migrant-caravan-mexico-photo-essay/, accessed December 14, 2018.

Watts, Jonathan. 2015. "Honduran Indigenous Rights Campaigner Wins Goldman Prize." *Guardian*, April 19. https://www.theguardian.com /world/2015/apr/20/honduran-indigenous-rights-campaigner-wins -goldman-prize, accessed December 31, 2017.

Watts, Jonathan. 2016. "Berta Cáceres, Honduran Human Rights and Environment Activist, Murdered." *Guardian*, March 4. https://www .theguardian.com/world/2016/mar/03/honduras-berta-caceres -murder-enivronment-activist-human-rights, accessed December 31, 2017.

Weinert-Kendt, Rob. 2016. "X Marks the Spot: Why We're Embracing Latinx." *American Theatre*, November 29. http://www.americantheatre .org/2016/11/29/x-marks-the-spot-why-were-embracing-Latinx/, accessed December 29, 2016.

Welch, Craig. 2018. "Why Cape Town Is Running Out of Water, and Who's Next." *National Geographic*, February 2. https://news .nationalgeographic.com/2018/02/cape-town-running-out-of-water -drought-taps-shutoff-other-cities/, accessed February 2, 2018.

Welsh, Teresa. 2017. "Hunger, Not Crime, Is Driving Central Americans to U.S. Border." *Miami Herald*, August 23. http://www.miamiherald.com /latest-news/article168957177.html, accessed December 10, 2017.

Wennersten, John R., and Denise Robbins. 2017. *Rising Tides: Climate Refugees in the Twenty-First Century*. Bloomington: Indiana University Press.

Wikipedia. "2014 American Immigration Crisis." en.wikipedia.org/wiki /2014_American_immigration_crisis.

Wilkie, Alex, Martin Savransky, and Marsha Rosengarden, eds. 2017. *Speculative Research: The Lure of Possible Futures*. London: Routledge.

Williams, Patricia. 1997. *Seeing a Color-Blind Future: The Paradox of Race*. New York: Noonday.

Windell, Maria A., and Jesse Alemán, eds. 2018. "Latinx Lives in Hemispheric Context." *English Language Notes (ELN)* 56, no. 2 (October).

World Health Organization. 2018. "List of Blueprint Priority Diseases."
     February. http://www.who.int/blueprint/priority-diseases/en/,
     accessed May 11, 2018.

Wulf, Andrea. 2016. *The Invention of Nature: Alexander von Humboldt's
     New World*. New York: Vintage Books.

Yale University Library. 2016. http://guides.library.yale.edu/c.php?g=
     512493&p=3506447, accessed December 29, 2016.

Ybarra, Patricia A. 2017. *Latinx Theater in the Times of Neoliberalism*.
     Evanston, Ill.: Northwestern University Press.

Ybarra, Priscilla Solis. 2016. *Writing the Goodlife: Mexican American
     Literature and the Environment*. Tucson: University of Arizona Press.

Yeo, Sophie. 2018. "How to Protect Rare Books and Manuscripts from
     the Ravages of Climate Change." *Pacific Standard*, May 11. https://
     psmag.com/environment/saving-our-archives-from-climate-change,
     accessed May 11, 2018.

Yoder, Kate. 2017. "From Hotumn to Meatmares: The Words that Defined
     Our Planet This Year." *Grist*, December 22. http://grist.org/article
     /from-hotumn-to-meatmares-the-words-that-defined-our-planet-this
     -year/, accessed December 22, 2017.

(Continued from page iii)

Shannon Mattern
Deep Mapping the Media City

Steven Shaviro
No Speed Limit: Three Essays on Accelerationism

Jussi Parikka
The Anthrobscene

Reinhold Martin
Mediators: Aesthetics, Politics, and the City

John Hartigan Jr.
Aesop's Anthropology: A Multispecies Approach

Claudia Milian is associate professor and director of the Program in Latino/a Studies in the Global South at Duke University. She is author of *Latining America: Black-Brown Passages and the Coloring of Latino/a Studies.*